WATERTON AND NORTHERN GLACIER
TRAILS
FOR HIKERS AND RIDERS

By: Charles Russell, Beth Russell,
John Russell and Valerie Haig-Brown

1995
Waterton Natural History Association

COVER PICTURES
Pack train on Sage Pass; hiker in Upper Waterton Valley; Wood Lily *(lilium philadelphium* bighorn ram. **BACK** - Stoney Indian Pass area.

ISBN 0-920457-04-5

Produced by Graphcom Printers Ltd., Lethbridge, Alberta

Printed and bound in Canada

Published by
Waterton Natural History Association
P.O. Box 145
Waterton Park, Alberta, T0K 2M0
1-403-859-2624

ACKNOWLEDGEMENTS

The Waterton Natural History Association is a non-profit organization working in cooperation with Parks Canada to further understanding and appropriate use of Waterton Lakes National Park. Together the WNHA and Employment and Immigration Canada have sponsored and funded this project through a Canada Works Grant administered by Robert Boycott.

This publication is the result of the cooperation and combined effort of many people whom we would like to thank for their help and advice. From Waterton Park, Duane Barrus, Terry Hammell, Larry Harbidge, Bernie Lieff, Simon Lunn, Randall Schwanke and Max Winkler, and in Glacier, Bob Frausen, Clyde Lockwood, Dick and Ursula Mattson, and David Shea were extremely helpful. Many thanks are also extended to: Dee Barrus, Burton V. Coale, David Cruikshank, Peggy Dixon, Betty Gamble, Ken Goble, John and Fran Jackson, David Hamer, Joy Lieff, David McNeill, Dianne Pachal, Dick Russell, Margaret Russell, Keith Shaw, Yvonne Stotyn, Patricia Wagenaar and Doris Wellman. Wendy Judd of Diamond Hitch Outfitters provided the front cover photograph of a pack train.

Patricia Benson of Parks Canada Western Regional Office assisted greatly with the maps, and secured the base map which was supplied by the Land Resource Research Institute, Research Branch, Agriculture Canada, Ottawa. We have adapted and up-dated the maps for this book. Copies of the full scale map are available from the Canada Map Office, your local map dealer or the Waterton Natural History Association.

We hope this book will provide many users of the Waterton-Glacier trails with definitive information to enhance their experiences in the Park.

We would like to thank Janice Smith and her colleagues in the Canadian Parks Service for their generous help with the updating required for the 1991 edition of this guide. Our thanks, too, to R. C. Harris of the Vancouver Natural History Society for his comments, particularly with regard to the B.C. sections.

And to all those who have used and enjoyed the Guide since 1984 and been so complimentary, we thank you and wish you continued happy hiking with this new edition. To those who are new to the Guide, may you enjoy Waterton and its trails as much as we do.

THE AUTHORS

CONTENTS

Travois Trail. Waterton is a rich archeological area.

FOREWORD

The trails of Waterton and Northern Glacier represent some of the most scenic in all our National Parks. They lead visitors through a wide variety of geography from the shores of the main lake up through the trees to timberline meadows and along high ridges over 2,750 metres above sea-level, where one can see a vast panorama of mountains tempered by the distant view of the flat rim of the prairie to the east. There is no comparable place in Canada with the spectrum of color or the contrast in topography.

The historic significance of these trails reaches from the most recent, only a few years old, to the ancient Indian South Kootenai Trail leading west up Pass Creek (Blakiston) over the the Continental Divide just an hour's walk south of Twin Lakes. How many thousand years this trail was used by native people before the white man ever saw it is anybody's guess. Certainly it was one of the most heavily travelled tracks before and after the Indians acquired horses.

It was the major route taken by Flathead and Kootenai tribes coming east to hunt buffalo and by the Blackfeet going from the plains to raid those tribes west of the Rockies.

Kootenai Brown used this trail on his first journey into this region coming east from the Flathead Valley in 1865. He later became the first acting superintendent of the Park, died here, and is buried on the north shore of Knight's Lake (Lower Waterton).

Bert Riggall, the first guide and outfitter of this region, even before the Park was officially inaugurated in 1910, was involved with exploring and cutting some of the trails still in use. Such men as Bo Holroyd, Mac McAllister, Wallace Gladstone and Chris Christianson, to name just a few of the earlier Park Wardens, surveyed and opened more of the present day trails. Over the years prior to World War II, these men patrolled the trails on horseback and snowshoes, summer and winter.

Forty-eight years ago, when I first began using the Park trails as a licensed guide, it would be most unusual if we saw a dozen people in the high country apart from our own guests over a two-week pack train trip. Now, if you take a horse, it will likely be on a day trip, for an overnight excursion requires carrying feed for saddle and pack animals.

So hiking is the most popular way of seeing the many beauties of the backcountry and, where there was just a few twenty years ago, now thousands are enjoying the trails. Properly planned and equipped, such a trip can be a very enjoyable and rewarding experience. Through sunshine and storm, there are few more beautiful places in the entire world as one follows mountain paths past vistas of peaks, streams and lakes, where wildflowers bloom in profusion and many kinds of wildlife can be observed in what is one of nature's finest and most diversified natural museums.

Good hiking and please keep your camps and the trails clean.

- *Andy Russell*

HOW TO USE THIS BOOK

 Picture keys (see next page) identify trail details.

Trailhead: Where the trail begins.

Destination: Where the trail ends.

Length: Includes both distance and time. Distances are given in both kilometres and miles. Times are provided as a guide only and are based on 15 minutes per kilometre on level ground, 30 minutes per kilometre for uphill hiking. You may complete a trail in more or less time depending on your ability and interests.

Difficulty Level: Easy trails are relatively flat. Moderately easy trails gain some elevation. Moderately difficult trails have difficult sections, such as rock or scree, and considerable uphill travel. Difficult terrain requires Registration for a Hazardous Activity Permit issued by a Park warden and demands mountain-climbing skills.

TRAIL PROFILE GRAPHS

These appear on all but easy trails. Each graph represents a cross-section of the terrain the trail covers, and elevations are accurately tied to distances. The graph should be considered together with the Difficulty Level to discern the physical demands of each trail.

ACCESS Describes the information necessary to reach the trailhead and lists alternatives where they exist.

ATTRACTIONS Highlights special features along the trail.

CONSIDERATIONS Identifies important preparations and situations. Read this section carefully!

THE TRAIL Offers a brief walk-along narrative of the trail itself with occasional information on the natural history of the area.

PICTURE KEY LEGEND

Throughout this book, picture keys are used to identify categories. As they appear on individual trail descriptions, picture keys provide a quick identification of the facilities and activities offered, as well as specific information about the trail.

Hiking Trails

Short Easy Walks

Horseback Riders

Backcountry Camping

Frontcountry Campgrounds

Picnic Area

Kitchen Shelter

Toilets (dry)

Horse Camping

Boat Dock – day use

Boat Launch

Information

First Aid

Telephone

Warden/Ranger Station

International Boundary – identifies road and trails that cross the Canada - U.S. border

Weather – identifies trails especially vulnerable to fast-changing mountain weather conditions

Charter Boats – provide water taxi service to lakeshore trails

Fishing

Swimming

Scuba Diving

Viewpoint

Tennis

Playground

 Wildlife

 Environmental Impact - identifies trails particularly susceptible to environmental damage if abused (e.g. short-cutting). Please be considerate.

 Post Office

 Disabled Use

 Winter Use

 Nordic Skiing

 Interpretive Trail

 Cycling

 Interpretive Hike

 Interpretive Theatre. Check with Information Bureau for locations, times and topics.

 Automobile Access - identifies points that require vehicle transportation.

 Bus Transportation

 Townsite Services

 Public Showers

 Fuels

 Motorless Boats

ORIGIN OF THE MOUNTAINS

It is often easier to understand and appreciate the present by looking into the past. The mountains of Waterton-Glacier provide not only a breath-taking sight, but a story written over billions of years in stone and water.

A thousand million years ago, this area was a flat open plain covered by a shallow inland sea. Layer upon layer of sediments were distributed on the bottom of this sea by surrounding rivers and streams. Over millions of years, these sedimentary layers compressed into rock as new layers were distributed atop old, eventually reaching a depth of as much as 10,000 metres.

About 100 million years ago, a great geological upheaval completely changed this terrain. In a process known as plate tectonics, a massive section of the earth's crust, the Pacific Plate, moved eastwards, colliding with the North American Plate. The impact of this gigantic collision forced the thick sedimentary layers to buckle and fold, forming the mountains that are today's Rockies.

In some areas, huge blocks of the sedimentary rock were forced up and over others. Known as overthrusting, this created unusual depositional sequences of older layers, often in millions of years, resting atop younger ones. In Waterton-Glacier, this geological phenomenon is quite visible. The Lewis Overthrust here presents an extensive example of these out-of-sequence layers. It is also the significant factor in Waterton's impressive combination of mountain and prairie landscape as one block of layers pushed out over another, creating mountains that rise abruptly from the open prairie.

Glaciation was the next force to sculpt this region. Although there are no glaciers presently in Waterton Park, the last vestiges of that era still exist in Glacier. Ice on remote Vulture Peak there melts to form the headwaters of the Waterton system of lakes and rivers. Glaciers began in a period of cooling temperatures when snowfields remained year-round on protected mountainsides and gradually compressed to form ice fields. With sufficient build-up, the ice began to move out of the upper valleys to join larger glaciers that had formed in Waterton and Belly River valleys which then carved their way out on to the prairies.

At least four glacial periods gouged and shaped the mountains here. Eventually the ice receded, leaving the mountains much as you see them today. The effects of glaciation are still vivid throughout Waterton-Glacier. The jagged teeth of Porcupine Ridge, at the southwest end of Waterton Lake, are the remains of a mountain attacked by glaciers from opposite sides. Wide U-shaped valleys such as Waterton and Blakiston were the routes of major glaciers and the cirques and hanging valleys such as Upper Rowe and Lineham Basin were created by the activity of smaller glaciers. Bare rock surfaces in many parts of Waterton-Glacier show the scars and scrape marks of passing glaciers.

Warming temperatures ended the glacial period and as the ice melted, massive ice blocks were left stranded in the valley bottoms. These blocks melted to form large lakes, such as Middle Waterton.

Tons of debris carried by the meltwaters from the side valleys formed constricting deltas that eventually created Waterton's chain of lakes. Today both wind and water, in its various forms, continue the evolution of this mountain terrain.

Waterton-Glacier's geological history has created a world where mountains of ancient sedimentary rock meet directly with prairie grasslands, creating a combination of prairie flora and fauna in close contact with mountain lifeforms. The mountains are weather-makers, catching the westerly air flow from the Pacific and creating variations in climate and unique wind conditions. Climate, elevation and terrain produce a varied habitat for the diverse range of species that inhabit Waterton and Glacier Parks today.

THE SEASONS

The seasons in Waterton-Glacier are as dramatic as the country itself. Although most visitors find their way here during the summer months, more people are discovering Waterton has much to offer year-round.

Spring   Although not all businesses and facilities are open, and the high country is still deep in snow, spring is an exciting time here. Sightseers enjoy the large herds of deer and elk that are commonplace on the greening flatlands along the entrance road, and Waterton townsite often has more mountain sheep on the streets than people. Only lowland trails are open in early spring, but they are not yet busy and hiking them is a peaceful pleasure.

Waterton valley is a main migration corridor for hundreds of species of waterfowl and songbirds. Ice-free lakes in the Park are a resting place for water birds from early April. Canada geese, and mallard, goldeneye and canvasback ducks join both whistler and trumpeter swans that congregate here. The brilliant flash of the mountain bluebird is a sure sign of the return of the songbirds. Warblers, sparrows and flycatchers soon follow. In all, 230 species of birds have been identified in this mountain and prairie habitat. Bird songs fill the air as mating and territorial changes take place. The leaves are still new and allow good visibility for bird-watching. Late spring can be a wet season, as rain or spring snow is precipitated from moist Pacific air flowing over the mountains. This combined with melting snow from the mountains provides high water in area rivers for canoeing and kayaking that are at their best in the spring.

For most, the Park officially opens on Victoria Day in late May when both townsite businesses and Waterton and Glacier park facilities welcome visitors for another summer season.

Summer   The mountains are at their best in July and August and Waterton townsite buzzes with activity. The gentler winds of summer and the beauty of mountain and lake attract colorful windsurfers while warm summer evenings are perfect for scenic lake excursions from the townsite marina. At Goat Haunt ranger station Northern Glacier Park personnel greet arriving boats. All trails are open and the high country beckons.

For many, summer is the flower season. The early lupin blue of lowland valleys soons gives way to the reds, pinks and yellows of gaillardia, locoweed and horse mint. The colorful show of wildflowers (over 800 species grow here, including 22 varieties of orchids) follows the retreating snow as summer reaches the high country.

Hikers and horseback riders use the long days to explore far into the alpine regions. The high mountain world comes alive as plants and animals take advantage of the short summer to rejuvenate, propagate and prepare for winter that soon returns.

Fall Summer's long days soon give way to the the long shadows of fall. But for many people, this is the perfect time to visit. The color of Waterton in autumn is gold – from the prairie grasslands baked by the hot summer sun to the larches high on the timberline. The days are still warm, but the morning and evening chill speaks of the changing season. Elk and deer return to the lowlands to join with moose in the fall display of antlers and gleaming winter coats. The bull elk gather their harems for the rutting season and their shrill bugling echoes through the valleys. Flocks of migrating waterfowl return southward through the Waterton Valley. Most visitors leave after Labor Day, but good weather will find several businesses open into October. Berries ripen along all-but-deserted trails. The alpine weather becomes unpredictable and snow is likely even at lower elevations.

Winter Waterton is quiet in winter, but for those who visit here there are several ways to enjoy the snowy wilderness. A few facilities remain open for winter visitors. The campsite at Blakiston Creek accommodates winter campers; enclosed kitchen shelters at Emerald Bay and on Waterton Avenue in Waterton townsite are supplied with firewood for winter warmups. Look for the snowflake picture key that identifies areas open for winter use.

Deer, elk and bighorn sheep winter ranges attract sightseers while climbers are drawn to the frozen waterfalls along the Akamina Parkway (13) for what is considered some of the finest ice climbing in the Rockies. Deep snow covers the alpine country and what are ideal summer trails become difficult and often dangerous winter mountaineering routes. Nordic skiing trailheads are concentrated along the Akamina Parkway. Winter is Waterton's windiest season and from November through February the winds can reach hurricane force. Waterton winters are also subject to Chinook winds. A warm westerly flow, Chinooks can blow in and melt the entire lower elevation snow cover in a matter of hours.

 # INFORMATION

There is much to know about these mountainous national parks and a number of groups and individuals are available to answer questions. In Waterton Lakes National Park, the main source of information and one that every park visitor should investigate is the Information Bureau. Located across from the Prince of Wales Hotel, the Bureau is open daily through July and August and limited hours in May, June and September. Phone (403) 859-2224. The staff here have a variety of free maps and brochures as well as details on weather and trail conditions, boat schedules, interpretive hikes and programs, and necessary Park permits. Radio contact with other Park services is maintained from the Bureau and it is the most direct point for contacting Park wardens. The park warden service may also be reached by telephone at (403) 859-2224.

The Waterton Natural History Association has available Park topographical maps, fishing licences and a number of Park-related publications in the Information Bureau.

A year-round information outlet is located in the Park administration office across from the Tamarack Mall. Open during week day business hours, this office may be reached at (403) 859-2224.

Park staff are trained and knowledgeable about the specifics of Waterton Park and are willing to answer your questions or assist in any way. The Waterton Chamber of Commerce and individual business people can also assist with townsite information.

For details on Glacier National Park, check with the Information Bureau and see Glacier (50).

THE TRAILS

Waterton-Glacier International Peace Park offers over 1280 km (900 mi.) of backcountry hiking trails that explore its varying terrain. Trails meander across Great Plains prairie and scramble to the top of razor-backed ridges. Others cross semi-arid regions, travel past waterfalls and through lush forests. Some follow ancient travel routes through glacier-carved valleys. A rich cross-section of plant and animal species occupy this diverse landscape and travel here can be a rewarding exchange with nature.

 Interpretive Trails

Some of Waterton's trails are self-guided interpretive walks. Signs along the Red Rock Canyon Loop (29) give information on the vegetation, geology and wildlife in the area. Pamphlets are available for the Lower Bertha Falls Trail (7) and are sold at the Heritage Centre, the Park's Information Centre and at the trailhead.

 Interpretive Hikes

Throughout the summer various educational programs offer visitors an opportunity to learn more about the flora and fauna. One such offering, the International Peace Park Hike, is jointly sponsored by both Parks. Interpreters from each country lead hikers along the Lakeshore Trail (9) and examine the continuity of the landscape in the world's first International Peace Park. Check with the Waterton Park Information Bureau for a complete schedule of times and topics for programs. Consult the Park newspaper.

During winter months, interpretive programs are available to Park visitors upon request. Phone (403) 859-2275 for more information. Check with the Administration Office for winter schedules.

 Nordic Skiing

Waterton Park maintains a number of Nordic ski tracks. A pamphlet describing Waterton's Nordic skiing opportunities and skiing conditions is available from the Park Administration office. Ski conditions can change radically in a short period and drifting snow can close access roads.

FOR YOUR SAFETY

Mountain Travel may be a new experience and, while the landscape is enticing, it can also be dangerous. You are responsible for your safety, but a few guidelines may assist you.

1. Pre-trip preparation is important. Review the trail and terrain you plan to explore and prepare accordingly.

2. Many higher elevation trails traverse rocky slopes. Caution is advised on steep terrain near trails. Most rock in Waterton-Glacier is sedimentary and often referred to as "rotten". Loose scree slopes, cliffs and boulder fields deserve consideration. Snow and avalanche deposits on many alpine and subalpine trails last well into summer. Free brochures available at the Information Bureau give useful tips and advice for hikers and riders.

3. Mountain travel is strenuous; trails are rarely level and elevation gain may be rapid. Explore shorter trails first and work up to longer ones. Remember that backpacking is best done at a slow even pace that gives the body a chance to adjust and allows time to enjoy the surroundings.

4. Hiking alone is not recommended.

5. In Waterton, pets are not encouraged on trails and must be kept on a leash. In Glacier, no pets are allowed on backcountry trails.

6. Most trails are open to both hikers and horseback riders. Good etiquette is expected of both parties. Horses have the right-of-way on trails and hikers should step to the side and quietly allow horses to pass.

7. Trails are generally well marked and clearly defined for easy backcountry navigation. However, natural occurrences and man-made improvements can change trails and their current conditions should be checked before starting out. Some trails are in areas where it is difficult to clearly define a path (tall grass, rocky slopes, etc.). These are usually marked with yellow or orange trail posts. Rock cairns are used on bare ground above treeline. In wooded areas, trail markers may be small signs on trees and, on remote routes, blazes may be used.

8. Routes are seldom-used trails that are neither maintained nor signed by Park staff. Hikers and riders should contact the Park warden service before considering travel along such routes.

Wood Ticks are present in Waterton-Glacier. Most active in spring, ticks are disease carriers and you should check for them after any hike. Careful inspection of your head, neck and abdomen usually reveals any ticks present. If a tick is attached and the area is not inflamed, slowly remove it and disinfect the area. If the area becomes inflamed, contact a physician.

 Weather

Mountain weather is unpredictable. Snow, sleet and freezing rain can occur with little notice even on the hottest days of summer. At lower levels this can be a minor annoyance or even a refreshing treat, but at higher elevations these conditions can be a serious problem if hikers or riders are not prepared. Many trails are above the treeline and offer little or no protection from precipitation or wind. Lightning, a common phenomenon in mountain storms, is a serious danger to exposed hikers, especially if laden with metal-framed packs.

Waterton is the windiest area in Alberta, and the wind here must always be taken into consideration when planning a hike. Velocities can be extreme on high mountain slopes and passes; it is generally wise to avoid these high places altogether on windy days.

Low cloud or fog also makes travel in high country difficult as landmarks may be impossible to see. Be prepared to retreat to lower elevations in case of changing weather.

The weather picture key identifies those trails where weather conditions are a major consideration.

Keep an eye on the scenery *and* the weather.

Mountain Waters Although beautiful and inviting, the water of Waterton and Glacier is extremely cold. Most are the meltwaters of glacial ice and snow and remain frigid throughout the year. Streams and rivers here are swift, especially during spring and summer run-off. A thin colorless algae that often covers rocks along shorelines and streambeds is extremely slippery; approach edges of streams and waterfalls with care.

For many, drinking from a cold stream is part of the mountain experience. Unfortunately, the possibility exists that some of these waters may be contaminated. The microscopic organism, *Giardia lamblia,* may be present in surface water and, if ingested, can cause serious problems. Diarrhea, nausea and severe stomach cramps are all possible effects and can be debilitating, especially in the back-country. The lower the elevation, the more likely that the water will be contaminated. Carrying water from a safe source is the best way to avoid the problem, but boiling natural water will destroy the organism.

Many trails have dry sections. Thirst, combined with a strenuous hike, can be very unpleasant. A container of water can save the day.

Hypothermia One of the most serious threats to mountain travellers and the least understood or prepared for is hypothermia. A cooling of the body temperature, hypothermia can lead to rapid physical and mental collapse and even death. Contributing factors are cold, wetness, wind chill, fatigue and lack of proper food. Add to any one of these the demanding physical exertion of alpine backpacking and hypothermia becomes a critical concern. You can slip into a hypothermic condition in a matter of minutes, especially when you stop moving, and victims may not be aware that they are in danger. Initial symptoms include persistent shivering; slow, slurred speech; and/or loss of coordination, especially in the hands. Memory lapse, incoherence and impaired judgement may also occur. If hypothermia becomes apparent warm the victim and get them to a sheltered location. Exchange any wet clothing for dry and get the victim into a sleeping bag with another person (skin-to-skin contact is most effective). Warm drinks and sweets can help.

Adequate preparation is the best method for avoiding this potential danger. Get plenty of rest and eat well before your hike. Carry extra clothing and some wet weather protection. If you do get wet, dry off fast. Use common sense and turn back if conditions are bad; there will be a better day.

BEARS

Grizzly and black bears once lived all over North America, but grizzlies particularly were so feared by settlers that they have been wiped out in all but a few places. Waterton-Glacier remains excellent bear habitat; they live here undisturbed most of the time. You can spend many days in the Parks without ever seeing a bear of either species or you may be lucky enough to see two or three from a distance, perhaps a mother and cubs.

Black and grizzly bears differ in appearance and it is wise to know the difference since their behaviour in an encounter will not be the same. Black bears are not always black – they may range through all the shades from blond to black and their muzzle may differ in color from their body. Black bears have short claws and can climb trees easily.

Grizzly bears are generally larger than black bears and have a hump at the shoulder which is a great mass of muscle. Grizzlies have long claws for digging. These claws are not really suitable for climbing trees, but grizzlies can still hoist themselves up a tree much the way we do if the branches are strong enough. Grizzlies also vary in color from blond to nearly black and one bear may have several shades of fur. Both species swim well.

Grizzly and black bears have similar diets and habits, although the grizzly is generally found more in open areas and the black is more likely in forested areas. Grizzly bears obtain much of their food by digging with their long front claws. Black bears rarely dig for food. Grizzlies eat roots, corms, bulbs, ground squirrrels and other underground food as well as the same green vegetation and berries that black bears eat. Both species feed on carrion and both are proficent hunters of vulnerable prey such as rodents or young elk or mountain sheep, although their diet is 90 percent vegetation.

The probability of a serious encounter with a bear is very low, but precautions are appropriate if this risk is to be kept to a minimum. Precautions focus on two major themes:

1. Control of availability of food and garbage odors. This includes leaving absolutely no food or garbage behind for the sake of those who may come after you.
2. Hike alertly and warn bears of your presence by making noise, especially in areas where visibility is restricted. Remember that bears can be met anywhere in the Parks, even in well-used picnic sites, on busy roadsides or on short well-used trails.

Details on dealing with bear encounters should be obtained from the Park staff at the Information Bureau or Administration Office and by reading the Park pamplet *You Are In Bear Country*.

Watching a bear from a distance is a most enjoyable experience. Both blacks and grizzlies may be viewed safely from your car on the Akamina and Red Rock parkways. Bears may be seen any time of day from either road, but the best times are the first and last hour of daylight. Look on open slopes and avalanche tracks on the mountainsides on either side of the road. If you happen to see a bear near the road **do not** get out of your car for any reason. It is unlawful to feed or approach a bear, and very dangerous. Bears that become roadside or picnic area bums must often be destroyed; feeding a bear is probably sentencing it to death. Enjoy watching the bears through your car window or binoculars and leave them to enjoy their natural pursuits at a distance.

 EMERGENCY

Telephones are located throughout Waterton townsite, at the Information Bureau and at the main Park gate. Emergency phone numbers are:

Fire	859-2113	
R.C.M.P.	859-2244	
Ambulance	859-2636	(May - Sept.)
Wardens	859-2636	(Emergency only)

In areas with no telephone, contact any Park staff; many have vehicles equipped with radios. The entrance kiosk at Crandell Campground on Red Rock Parkway also has a radio. 911 does not apply.

 FIRST AID

Contact any park staff for directions when in need of assistance – many are first aiders.

EQUIPMENT

Clothing Like most outdoor activities, hiking requires special clothing. Style is not important on mountain trails, but proper clothing is – your life can depend on it and your comfort and enjoyment certainly do. A combination of cotton and wool in layers that can be shed or added to as conditions demand works best. Lowland summer weather may persuade you to start out in shorts, but temperatures drop approximately one degree for every 200 metres of elevation gain, and insects, brush and rocks can also prove long pants the most practical and comfortable.

Extra Clothing Weather changes fast in the mountains and being caught in cold, wet or wind can lead to hypothermia (see Hypothermia this section). An extra sweater, windbreaker, rain gear (even large garbage bags) and a wool toque (40 percent of body heat is lost through the head) are essential items for any hike.

Footwear Comfortable boots or shoes that are well broken in are essential. Good gripping soles are an important consideration. Hiking boots are preferable and provide ankle support for rock or steep inclines. Sneakers with good soles may be used on short easy trails and in dry snow-free areas. Blisters have ruined many a hike. Carry a small piece of moleskin or white adhesive tape to ease unexpected sore areas.

Backpack A comfortable backpack is necessary for the gear you will need and want to carry, even on short hikes.

Trail Food Hiking can be strenuous. High energy foods such as nuts, raisins and candy bars help to keep your energy level up. Always carry more food than you think you'll need!

Insect Repellent Although Waterton-Glacier is not known as fly country, mosquitos, deer flies and no-see-ums can be annoying company. Repellents help.

Maps Although this book includes maps, travellers, hikers and riders are advised to obtain the official Waterton and Glacier topographical maps. Available at the Information Bureau, townsite businesses and Northern Glacier ranger stations, your topographical map can be the most important item in your pack. It may be essential to the success of your trip, and it also makes good reading before and after your journey.

Other Essentials It is wise to carry a first aid kit and matches in a waterproof container. A knife, heavy string and gloves can prove invaluable. Although most hikes in Waterton can be easily completed in a day, some trails here and in Northern Glacier require overnight camping. For such hikes, a sleeping bag, ground mat, tent with rain fly and portable stove will be necessary. Good judgement and experience will help you make your own list of essentials.

CAMPING

  Front Country Campgrounds

Waterton's campground facilities are open to campers for a fee and are equipped to handle both tent campers and recreational vehicles. A reservation system is being developed.

The Townsite Campground in Waterton townsite (1) offers proximity to townsite facilities, easy access to Waterton lakeshore, and an interpretive theatre all in a stunning setting of mountain and lake. Serviced and unserviced sites together with a walk-in area accommodate most needs. Kitchen shelters, restrooms and public showers are also available. No open fires are permitted, and the area is quite exposed to the wind.

Crandell Campground on the Red Rock Parkway (26) offers a forest setting beside a mountain stream. Fireplaces here at individual unserviced sites create a backcountry atmosphere. Covered kitchen shelters, washrooms and water taps are convenient. An interpretive theatre presents nightly programs throughout the summer.

Belly River Campground located on the Chief Mountain International Highway (46) is set on the Belly River bank. From this small out-of-the-way campground, the wide valley of the river reaches back to the mountains of Glacier Park. Campsites are unserviced, but there are firegrates, kitchen shelters, toilets and tap water (boil first).

Group Camping is available at the Belly River Campground also. A protected open area accommodates large groups. Preference is given to non-profit groups of 35 or more and reservations are required. Contact Visitor Services, Waterton Lakes National Park (403) 859-2224.

Just outside the Park are the privately-owned Waterton Homestead and Waterton Riverside Campgrounds, as well as the Crooked Creek Campground owned by the Waterton Natural History Association which offers primitive camping.

 Backcountry Camping

Waterton maintains fourteen backcountry campsites, and a stay at any of these can greatly enhance your visit. To use backcountry campsites, a $5/site permit must be obtained from the Information Centre. There is a limit to the number of people each site can accommodate. A backcountry reservation system is being developed and may be operational. Otherwise permits are given on a first-come, first-served basis. Please inquire at the Information Centre or call (403) 859-2224. July and August weekends are busiest. Maps and information are available at the Information Centre which give details of the location, facilities and restrictions for each campsite.

Designated campsites have dry toilets. Some may have kitchen shelters and firegrates for campfires and cooking. Open fires may not be permitted at all designated backcountry campsites. Hazardous fire conditions and lack of firewood make portable stoves the most practical and preferred means of cooking in the backcountry.

Backcountry camping at Lineham Lakes Basin (15) is an exception. Campsites there remain undesignated in an effort to reduce impact on the fragile environment. There are no facilities and no fires are permitted.

In all backcountry campsite areas, always observe good housekeeping. Pack out all that you pack in and keep mountain waters clear of pollution by washing dishes and yourself in water that you have carried well away from the stream or lake. Use biodegradable soap and empty water away from its source. Consult the *You Are in Bear Country* pamphlet for suggested precautions while camping in mountain parks.

FISHING

From high alpine lakes to rushing trout streams to peaceful beaver ponds, Waterton and Glacier National Parks offer a wide variety of fishing. Cutthroat, rainbow and brook trout inhabit many of the high lakes and may also be found, along with whitefish, northern pike, lake trout, Dolly Varden and other species, at lower elevations. Fishing seasons vary through Waterton-Glacier, as do conditions, and it is best to check with the Information Bureau before setting out. Here you may obtain the National Parks fishing license necessary in Waterton, a copy of the Park fishing regulations and B.C. fishing licenses for points west of the Divide.

Requirements for fishing in Glacier National Park vary from those in Waterton; see Glacier (50).

Please adhere to limit restrictions so fish populations may be maintained for future enjoyment. Always properly dispose of fish entrails and contain fish odors that might otherwise attract bears. Plastic bags are available from the Information Bureau.

HORSEBACK RIDERS

Travelling horseback has long been both a practical and pleasant way of seeing Waterton-Glacier Parks. Indians and explorers used horses and many of the park trails were first blazed with pack trains in mind. Today, riding remains a popular activity.

Although Waterton-Glacier trails are well-graded, consideration must be given to the physical condition of your animal. Green, overweight horses can experience difficulty on any but the easiest trails and even well-conditioned animals require rest periods on switchbacks and steep inclines. Rocky sections require horses be properly shod. Avoid hazards by investigating questionable areas on foot and leading horses when necessary. Snow should be avoided altogether if at all possible. Help to minimize impact on delicate mountain terrtain by staying on designated trails and not riding two abreast. Grazing is not allowed in the parks; use pelletized horse feed.

Hiker-rider encounters are common and good relations require cooperation by both parties. Kindly ask hikers to step aside and stand quietly while you pass.

When unsaddling, use hitch rails where provided. If it is necessary to tie to a tree, choose one large enough to withstand rope damage and pad the rope. Securely restrain stock and store tack carefully. Salty sweat on equipment attracts animals and it is not uncommon to have a bridle carried off by a delighted deer or chewed by a porcupine. Scatter manure at rest stops and leave the area more pleasant for those who follow.

Horses are not permitted in Waterton townsite; however, the Townsite Bypass Trail (5) gives riders access to townsite trailheads. On individual trails, specific information of concern to riders is identified thus: **HORSES.** The rider picture key identifies those trails open to horseback riders.

 Horse Camping

Horses kept in the backcountry overnight must be kept in corrals provided by the park. These are located at Alderson Lake (10), Snowshoe Cabin (33) (with prior permission from the Warden Service) and Lone Lake (41). Grazing is not permitted. Horse feed must be packed in. Required camping permits are available at the Information Centre along with a few *Horse Use Guidelines* brochure.

Apart from backcountry camping, riders wishing to overnight in Waterton Park must make arrangements with Alpine Stables on the entrance road. Phone (403) 859-2462. The Stables provide both season and overnight boarding. Horses may also be rented here by the hour and Alpine Stables guides offer escorted rides throughout the Park. For additional information on horse use in Waterton contact the Park warden service (403) 859-2224. For horse use in Glacier Park, see Glacier Park (50).

 # ENVIRONMENTAL IMPACT

National parks are set aside to preserve a wilderness heritage. Waterton-Glacier's many trails provide access to country that would otherwise be inaccessible to most people. As you explore the wonders of the area remember, as powerful as these mountains regions appear, they are actually delicate environments. Those of us who are fortunate enough to find our way here must enjoy this beauty carefully. Trails are designed to allow the least possible impact on their surroundings. Please stay on the designated trails and do not use shortcuts as the resulting erosion has a devastating effect on this delicate terrain. Rules and regulations are not intended to create discomfort, but rather to insure the preservation of this area for future use and future generations.

Every visit by man changes this natural world in some way. Please be considerate of the environment; don't pick flowers or remove artifacts, antlers, rocks or other natural objects. Carry out all that you carry in. Enjoy yourself, but be aware of Waterton-Glacier's beautiful, vulnerable environment.

Boulder Pass.

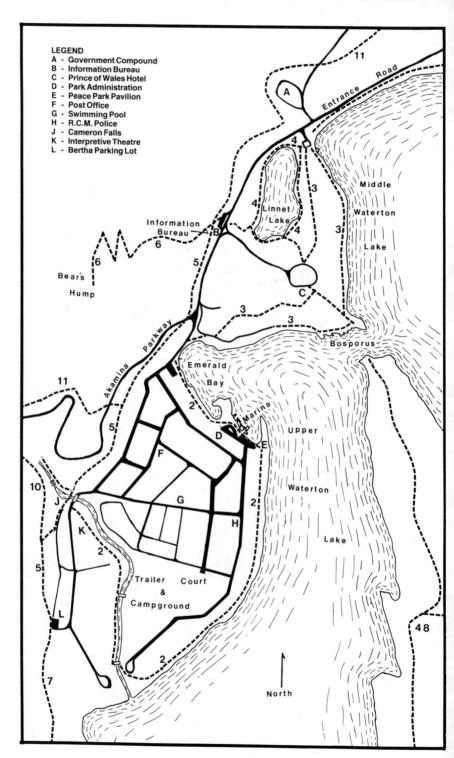

LEGEND
A - Government Compound
B - Information Bureau
C - Prince of Wales Hotel
D - Park Administration
E - Peace Park Pavilion
F - Post Office
G - Swimming Pool
H - R.C.M. Police
J - Cameron Falls
K - Interpretive Theatre
L - Bertha Parking Lot

WATERTON TOWNSITE

1 WATERTON TOWNSITE

TRAILHEAD FOR:
STROLLS AROUND TOWN – Townsite (2), Prince of Wales (3), Linnet Lake, (4), Townsite Bypass (5) trails.
HIKES FROM THE TOWNSITE – Bear's Hump (6), Lower Bertha Falls (7), Bertha Lake (8), Lakeshore (9), Alderson Lake (10), Crandell Mountain Loop (11), and boat service for Crypt Lake (12).

In many ways, Waterton townsite is like the alpine meadows high above this tiny town. During the winter months, the townsite is almost dormant. Winds off the frozen lake can pile huge snowdrifts in the town and most cottages and businesses are boarded up for protection. Mule deer and bighorn sheep roam the empty streets and bed down in the lee of vacant cottages. Although the Park is open all year, as few as a hundred residents call Waterton home year-round. A two-room school accommodates local children, and a handful of businesses remain open to welcome Nordic skiers and those who venture here to enjoy the beauty of Waterton in winter. As spring awakens and warming temperatures melt the snow, the townsite begins to stir. More and more visitors appear, and the shops and businesses shed their protective coverings. By the Victoria Day weekend, most facilities are open.

A wide range of services are available and include: hotels and motels, restaurants and gas stations, grocery and gift stores, a cinema, drug store, banking facilities, and a coin laundry. Several religious denominations offer services throughout the summer and government facilities include an R.C.M.P. detachment, a post office and a liquor store.

Many Park facilities are located in the townsite. Important to all visitors is the Information Centre located at the top of the hill opposite the drive into the Prince of Wales Hotel. Staff here can advise and suggest many things to see and do in the Park as well as provide necessary permits and informative publications. An Interpretive Theatre near Cameron Falls presents nightly features on Waterton's natural history. The Park Administration Office is located on Mount View road near the Marina and the Warden/Interpreter Offices are situated in the government compound across from the Linnet Lake parking lot.

Enjoyment of the townsite is enhanced by its recreational facilities. Waterton Park's largest campground (equipped with public showers) is here, as well as tennis courts, a playground and a solar heated swimming pool. Cameron Falls and the International Peace Park Pavilion are but two of the many features explored along a network of easy trails around the town. Longer hikes extend to the surrounding mountains. Well-placed picnic sites, several of which are enclosed for year-round use, invite visitors to enjoy the striking scenery. Emerald Bay is a popular attraction. A sunken steamship lures scuba divers and the gentler breezes in this protected harbor provide a good launching area for windsurfers.

Emerald Bay Marina offers access to Waterton Lakes. Docking facilities are available for private boats and commercial services offer scenic excursions and water-taxi services for hikers. Public boat launches are provided west of the marina and at Linnet Lake parking lot.

Although a small town, Waterton Park offers all the basic services and introduces visitors to the beauty of Waterton Lakes National Park.

2 TOWNSITE TRAIL

Trailhead: Waterton Townsite
Destination: Loop around the townsite
Length: 3.2 km (2 mi.) allow 1 hr. around loop
Difficulty Level: Easy

ACCESS This trail circles the town on three sides and can be made a loop by connecting with the Townsite Bypass Trail (5) or returning to Cameron Falls along Evergreen Ave. It may be joined at any point in the townsite such as the Peace Park Pavilion, the marina area or Cameron Falls.

ATTRACTIONS Shoreline stroll, access to fishing from Victoria Day to Labor Day. Points of interest include Cameron Falls, Falls Interpretive Theatre, International Peace Park Pavilion, Emerald Bay Marina and Farmers Bay Beach. Good jogging trail.

CONSIDERATIONS Sections along lakeshore can be windy.

THE TRAIL Visitors to Waterton will find this stroll a pleasant way to acquaint themselves with the attractions of the townsite. A major natural feature on the route is Cameron Falls which drops over some of the oldest exposed rock in the Rocky Mountains, as much as 1.6 billion years old. From the Falls, the trail follows Cameron Creek downstream past the Interpretive Theatre. This indoor underground interpretive centre presents daily features. A wide range of free programs are offered; check at the Information Bureau for times and topics.

The trail meets Upper Waterton Lake near the mouth of Cameron Creek and is a good point for lake trout, rainbow and whitefish angling. Together with comfortable picnic sites, this is an ideal place to spend an enjoyable afternoon. The walk continues along the shoreline and offers sweeping views of Waterton Lake and its surrounding mountains. Ahead, the International Peace Park Pavilion sits on a small peninsula that shields Emerald Bay from the lake winds. Built and dedicated in 1982, the Pavilion commemorates the 50th Anniversary of the Waterton-Glacier International Peace Park, the world's first such designation. The Pavilion celebrates the cooperation and peace between Canada and the United States and the reality that nature knows no political boundaries.

The trail continues along the docks of Emerald Bay Marina. Dock facilities are here for private vessels, and charter or tour boats offer service to destinations on the shores of Waterton Lake. Farmers Bay, a sandy beach just beyond the Marina, is popular with children. From Emerald Bay, you can complete the loop by returning along Evergreen Avenue or connect with the Townsite Bypass Trail (5) for a peaceful, wooded walk back to Cameron Falls. Mule deer (so-called for their long ears) and bighorn sheep use the townsite as part of their winter range and many stay on into the summer to enjoy the good grazing on cottage lawns.

3 PRINCE OF WALES

Trailhead:	Emerald Bay in Waterton townsite
Destination:	Loop trail returning to Emerald Bay
Length:	2 km (1.2 mi.) allow 3/4 hr. around loop
Difficulty Level:	Easy

ACCESS This trail may be approached from three points: the Emerald Bay picnic area, Linnet Lake parking lot or the Prince of Wales Hotel.

ATTRACTIONS Emerald Bay, an interesting lakeshore stroll. Access to fishing at the Bosporus (Narrows) from Victoria Day to Labor Day. Views of Waterton Valley from Prince of Wales hill.

CONSIDERATIONS Rocky section at the Bosporus can be very windy, wet and cold.

THE TRAIL This loop trail travels the lakeshore around the Prince of Wales hill and up to the picturesque Prince of Wales Hotel before descending back to the lakeshore at Emerald Bay. A popular area, Emerald Bay attracts visitors for its picnic facilities and peaceful view. Scuba divers congregate here to explore the sunken paddlewheel steamship that rests at the bottom of the bay. The trail heads east across the rocky beach below the Prince of Wales hill. Douglas fir trees here tell the story of the high winds for which Waterton is well known. Their stunted, twisted growth is living proof that Waterton is one of the windiest areas in Alberta. Although the average breeze is only 30 km/h, in the windy season from November to February winds greater than 175 km/h have been recorded.

Fishermen travel this trail to the Bosporus where the lake trout fishing is considered the best in the Park. In 1920, a 23 kg (51 lb.) trout was taken here, and in the past, Indians of the region used these narrows for trapping fish. From the Bosporus, the trail continues along the shore of Middle Waterton Lake to Linnet Lake. The scenic picnic site here invites travellers to enjoy this historic spot. Known as Moccasin Flats, this was a popular campsite for Indians and explorers. From Linnet Lake, the trail circles south and climbs to the Prince of Wales Hotel. This stately landmark of Waterton Park first opened its doors in 1927 and continues to attract visitors for the view, both inside and outside the lobby. From the hotel, the trail drops back down to Emerald Bay along a grassy hillside.

4 LINNET LAKE

Trailhead:	Waterton Townsite
Destination:	Loop around Linnet Lake
Length:	1 km (.6 mi.) allow ½ hr. around loop
Difficulty Level:	Easy

ACCESS The trail around Linnet Lake begins in the parking area across from the government compound. Linnet Lake is also a point of interest on the Prince of Wales Trail (3).

ATTRACTIONS Quiet, wooded walk near townsite. Graded and paved for handicapped use.

THE TRAIL A gentle, level trail, the Linnet Lake loop offers a quiet stroll after dinner or on a windy day, and is a good place to stretch your legs after a long drive. Lodgepole pine, Douglas fir, trembling aspen, birch and balsam poplar comprise the surrounding forest. The lake, called a kettle in geological terms, was formed when a block of ice, buried by glacial deposits, slowly melted away after the glaciers retreated. This peaceful trail was paved and levelled for the disabled as a 1985 Parks Canada Centennial Project.

5 TOWNSITE BYPASS

Trailhead: Information Centre, Waterton Townsite
Destination: Bertha Lake Trail (8) parking lot
Length: 1.3 km (.8 mi.) allow ½ hr. one way
Difficulty Level: Easy

ACCESS The Townsite Bypass Trail branches left (south) from the Bear's Hump Trail (6) directly above the Information Centre. This trail can also be reached from either side of Cameron Falls. **HORSES:** Riders approaching from the stables, cross to Crandell Loop Trail (11) and follow it south to the Bypass Trail.

ATTRACTIONS Peaceful, wooded path. Alternative trail around townsite.

CONSIDERATIONS Ticks in spring. Hikers please give right-of-way to horseback riders. **HORSES:** Riders must use the Bypass Trail for access to Alderson Lake (10), Bertha (7 and 8), and Lakeshore (9) trails as horses are not allowed on Waterton townsite streets. Horses may be trailered to the Bertha parking lot.

THE TRAIL The Townsite Bypass Trail skirts the western edge of Waterton townsite above and behind private cottages, and allows access to several trails while avoiding congestion in the town itself. From the Information Centre, the trail drops down and crosses the Akamina Parkway. It travels below the Parkway to the Crandell Mountain Loop Trail (11) which branches right (west). The Bypass Trail continues south through open forest before it drops down to meet Cameron Falls Drive at the falls, where it crosses the stream on a footbridge. The trail follows Alderson Lake Trail (10) briefly to the first switchback, where it branches left (south) to the Bertha Lake Trail parking area.

BEAR'S HUMP VIEW

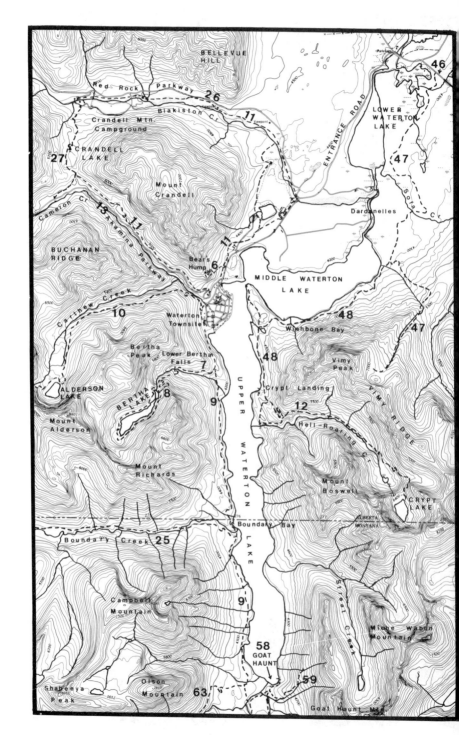

WATERTON VALLEY

30

6 BEAR'S HUMP

Trailhead:	Waterton Townsite
Destination:	Bear's Hump viewpoint
Length:	1.4 km (0.9 mi.) allow 40 min. one way
Difficulty Level:	Moderately difficult

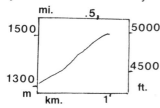

ACCESS The trail begins at the Information Bureau parking lot.

ATTRACTIONS Excellent view of Waterton townsite. A mini-mountain climb right from the edge of town.

CONSIDERATIONS A steep climb. Wind can be quite severe on top. Watch the edge, particularly with children. Rock may be slippery when wet. Do not throw rocks - you may endanger other hikers on the trail below or climbers who sometimes scale the rock face. Please stay on the trail and do not take shortcuts; the thin, rocky soil erodes easily. No facilities. Return by same route.

THE TRAIL This short but steep trail switchbacks up to a rocky ledge overlooking Waterton townsite. It takes some energy to climb over 200 metres in the space of only a kilometre, but the view makes the effort worthwhile. Pause awhile at the top with the toy-like townsite spread out below on an alluvial fan. The fan has grown over thousands of years as Cameron Creek washes sand, gravel and rocky debris into the lake. To the south, Upper Waterton Lake stretches between high mountain peaks into Montana; and, to the north is a contrasting view of Waterton's mountain-prairie contact. The wide U-shape of the Waterton valley reflects its glaciated past. The rock that forms this viewpoint perch was once part of a solid wall that extended across the valley bottom to the foot of Vimy Peak. During the ice age, glacial ice from the Upper Waterton Valley was contained behind this barrier. Eventually enough ice accumulated to flow over the wall, grinding it down to its present remains. As it flowed from its entrapment, this huge build-up of ice carved deeply into the valley bottom creating Upper Waterton Lake, the deepest lake in the Canadian Rockies at 120 metres.

7 LOWER BERTHA FALLS

Trailhead: Waterton Townsite
Destination: Lower Bertha Falls
Length: 2.9 km (1.8 mi.) allow 1 hr. one way
Difficulty Level: Moderately easy

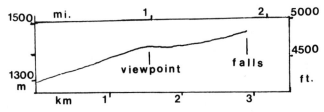

ACCESS The trail begins in a small parking lot south of Cameron Falls on Evergreen Avenue in Waterton townsite. **HORSES:** Unload here or use the Waterton Bypass Trail (5) to the Bertha trailhead.

ATTRACTIONS Lower Bertha Falls. One of Waterton's self-guided interpretive trails. Views of Waterton Lake.

CONSIDERATIONS About halfway to the Falls, two trails branch left; keep to the right. Picnic facilities are at the end of the trail near the Falls. Return by the same route. **HORSES:** To reach Bertha Falls, do not take the creek ford trail to Bertha Lake. Continue on the hiking trail to the Lower Falls where a hitch rail is provided. During the peak summer season, this trail is closed to horse use beyond the Lakeshore Trail (9) turnoff. Check at the Information Centre for details.

THE TRAIL The woodland walk to picturesque Lower Bertha Falls is easily done in half a day, but this self-guided nature trail makes a perfect day hike with a picnic and the children. The pamphlet *Bertha Falls Trail*, available at the trailhead, offer a basic course in Waterton's natural history. The trail is steepest as it rises above Upper Waterton Lake, but well-placed benches offer good rest stops for admiring the fine views of Waterton valley. At 1.5 km, a short spur trail branches left to a lookout, as the main trail continues to the right. About 50 metres beyond, the Lakeshore Trail (9) branches left (south), while the Bertha Falls Trail heads up the canyon high above Bertha Creek. Gradually the creek and the trail converge and you approach Lower Bertha Falls which tumble swiftly over bedrock that has been tilted to a 45-degree angle. Picnic here with the sound of rushing water. You may see a dipper wade down under the foam to find his lunch. The dipper, or water ouzel, resembles a large grey wren and constructs its nest of live moss on vertical cliffs, often in the spray of waterfalls.

8 BERTHA LAKE

Trailhead:	Waterton Townsite
Destination:	Bertha Lake
Length:	5.7 km (3.5 mi.) allow 3 hrs. one way
Difficulty Level:	Moderately difficult

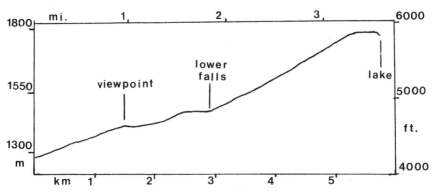

ACCESS This is a continuation of Lower Bertha Falls Trail (7). **HORSES:** Follow the horse ford trail which branches right 200 metres below Lower Bertha Falls to connect with Bertha Lake. Horses restricted during the months of July/August.

ATTRACTIONS Bertha, a high mountain lake in a hanging valley. Backcountry hike close to townsite. Fine views of Waterton Valley.

CONSIDERATIONS Steep grade. Take a lunch and your time. Return by same route. **HORSES:** The trail is steep on both sides of the stream ford. The ford is hazardous during high water as current is fast and runs through large boulders.

THE TRAIL The Bertha Lake Trail switchbacks up steep avalanche slopes and travels through cool coniferous forest to mile-long Bertha Lake nestled high in a mountain basin. The climb begins as soon as you leave the Lower Falls. The trail skirts an avalanche slope covered with springy alder shrubs, the only tree not crushed by the tons of snow that scour the steep north face of Mount Richards in winter. A subalpine forest of Engleman spruce, alpine fir and larch line the remainder of the trail. Occasional openings in the trees offer glimpses of Upper Bertha Falls which drop from the lip of the hanging valley above. A fine view greets your arrival at the lake -- Mount Richards to the left, Mount Alderson ahead and Bertha Peak to the right form this high cirque. To the right, the trail drops down to the lakeshore and the campsite facilities. Whether you stop to picnic, fish or hike the trail that circles the lake, keep an eye on the mountain slopes for the variety of wildlife that frequent this basin.

9 LAKESHORE

Trailhead: Waterton Townsite
Destination: Boundary Bay, International Boundary or Goat Haunt Ranger Station, Glacier Park.
Length: To Boundary Bay 5.8 km (3.6 mi.) allow 2 hrs. one way
To Goat Haunt 13 km (8 mi.) allow 3 to 4 hrs. one way.
Difficulty Level: Moderately easy

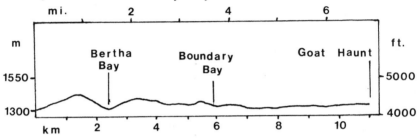

ACCESS The Lakeshore Trail leaves Waterton townsite along the Bertha Falls Trail (7). **HORSES:** Unload in the Bertha Lake Trail parking lot or use the Townsite Bypass Trail (5).

ATTRACTIONS Lakeside picnic and campsites at Bertha and Boundary bays. Moderately easy hike along the shore of Upper Waterton Lake. Orchid habitat. International interpretive hikes in July and August. Good lakeshore fishing from Victoria Day to Labor Day.

CONSIDERATIONS Hikers continuing to Goat Haunt will be subject to U.S. Immigration clearance; carry identification. Charter boat pick-ups from Boundary Bay or Goat Haunt can be arranged by prior reservation. Check with Information Bureau for fares and schedules. **HORSES:** Animals crossing the International Boundary must have proper medical certification. See Glacier Park (50). An overhanging ledge is encountered just beyond Bertha Bay and riders must lead their mounts.

THE TRAIL From Waterton townsite, the Lakeshore Trail follows the Bertha Falls Trail for 1.5 km before branching left and

heading south. It is a quick descent to Bertha Bay through lodgepole pine. Botanists and flower lovers will delight in the chance to see many of the 22 species of orchids that grow in Waterton along this section of the trail. A pleasant beach, camping facilities and a day-use boat dock make Bertha Bay an excellent objective only 2.4 km from the townsite. As it continues to Boundary Bay, the trail crosses rib-ridges running from Mount Richards to the lakeshore.

Boundary Bay has provision for both picnicing and camping, a day-use boat dock, and offers good fishing at the mouth of Boundary Creek. A stone cairn marks the International Boundary with the United States. Across the lake, a cutline running up the side of Mount Boswell represents the 49th parallel. This tiny slash is the only sign of the man-made border. Waterton-Glacier is the world's first International Peace Park, a designation that signifies the unity of the area's terrain and its flora and fauna. The designation also celebrates the friendship of Canada and the United States. Each Saturday from July to September, naturalists from both Waterton and Glacier jointly sponsor a day-long international hike along the length of this trail. Check with the Information Bureau for more details. Beyond Boundary Bay, the trail crosses Boundary Creek to the junction with Boundary Creek Trail (25).

The Lakeshore Trail continues south 5 km to Goat Haunt Ranger Station through mature forest. Return to Waterton by the same trail or by charter boat from Goat Haunt.

10 ALDERSON LAKE

Trailhead:	Waterton Townsite
Destination:	Alderson Lake
Length:	6.8 km (4.2 mi.) allow 2½ to 3 hrs. one way
Difficulty Level:	Moderately easy from Waterton

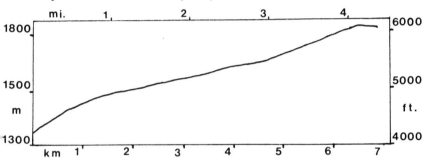

ACCESS From Waterton townsite the Alderson Lake Trail begins at the safety fence on the south side of Cameron Falls. **HORSES:** Use the Townsite Bypass Trail (5) for this access. If trailering animals, use the Bertha Trail parking lot (7). Alderson Lake can also be approached from Cameron Lake via the Carthew-Alderson Trail (24).

ATTRACTIONS The vertical north face of Mount Alderson. Alderson Lake cutthroat fishing. A well-treed valley path makes this a good hike on a windy day.

CONSIDERATIONS A steady uphill climb from Waterton. Return by same route. Approaching from Cameron Lake or continuing on to the Carthew-Alderson Trail beyond Alderson Lake requires a major summit crossing. See Carthew-Alderson Trail (24).

THE TRAIL Most of this trail offers a

sheltered walk through mature forests to Alderson Lake, nestled at the base of a 900-metre high cliff. As you leave the townsite at Cameron Falls and climb out of Waterton Valley, lodgepole pine and spruce forest line your path. Between the trees, you can peer into Cameron Creek gorge which is deeply carved into sedimentary rock. The trail climbs steadily and turns southwest up Carthew Creek Valley through mature Douglas fir and on into the subalpine zone where shrubs and alpine fir predominate. Near Alderson Lake, you cross a glacial moraine (debris left by a retreating glacier). This gravel ridge forms the dam that holds the lake. At 60 metres, Alderson is the deepest of Waterton's high lakes and with towering Mount Alderson behind, it is a spectacular sight. The tranquil lake surface is occasionally ruffled by rising cutthroat or downdrafts off the cliff. Camping facilities make this a good overnight spot, especially if you plan to continue over the summit to Cameron Lake on the Carthew-Alderson Trail.

11 CRANDELL LOOP

Trailhead: Waterton Townsite
Destination: Circuit of Mount Crandell
Length: 20.6 km (12.8 mi.) allow 6 to 8 hrs.
Difficulty Level: Moderately easy

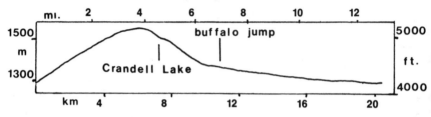

ACCESS The Crandell Mountain Loop Trail leaves Waterton townsite 400 metres south of Akamina Parkway on the Townsite Bypass trail (5). It can also be easily picked up at a number of points on its circular route, including Crandell Campground off the Red Rock Parkway (26) or the Crandell Lake trailhead on the Akamina Parkway (13). **HORSES:** Riders departing the Alpine Stables should cross the Park entrance road and join the trail above the government compound.

ATTRACTIONS Good horse trail. Low elevation makes this a good hike early in spring or on days with low cloud. Calypso orchids in June. Buffalo jump interpretive exhibit along the north side of the loop.

CONSIDERATIONS Trail closely parallels sections of the Akamina and Red Rock parkways. All facilities at Crandell Lake. Carry water. **HORSES and CYCLISTS:** Steep rocky sections and two stream crossings along the section from the townsite to Crandell Lake deserve attention. Even when dry, stream bed rocks are slippery. At Crandell Lake, tie horses away from campsite facilities and picnic areas.

THE TRAIL The trail crosses the Akamina Parkway, climbs quickly in the first kilometre and then ascends more

gradually, through pine and Douglas fir forest, above the roadway. Parts of the path have been blasted from limestone cliff on the steep side of Mount Crandell. Small waterfalls cool the air at intervals. At the pass into Blakiston Valley, the trail joins Crandell Lake Trail (27) through the basin. To continue the loop, at the end of the Lake Trail section bear left on a gravel road .4 km to cross the Blakiston Creek bridge and pick up the footpath that travels east (right) between the creek and Red Rock Parkway.

For the next several kilometres you are in a riparian (riverbank) environment. Below Crandell Campground, Blakiston is a braided stream lying in a wide bed of rock, gravel and clay eroded from its banks. In times of flood, as one channel fills, the water finds another, thus producing a braided effect. About .5 km east of the campground access road, the trail enters a heavy forest of cottonwood trees with their deeply cracked bark. Rising above the stream, the trail climbs high banks carved from an aggregate of clay and gravel known as glacial till. These steep banks were used by Indians as a buffalo jump for thousands of years. An interpretive display explains their techniques.

Further on the stream has undercut a high bank of pink-colored till on its far side. **HORSES:** During low water, riders may wish to ford the creek just downstream from this bank and follow a trail behind the golf course and past Lonesome Lake to the townsite. Hikers should continue on the east side of the the creek opposite the golf course. The golf course butts against a ridge coming down off Mount Crandell which is the huge moraine formed where the Blakiston and Waterton valley glaciers merged.

Proceed to the Park entrance road and cross the creek on the bridge. From here, follow a path just to the right of the road back to the townsite.

12 CRYPT LAKE

Trailhead:	Crypt Landing
Destination:	Crypt Lake
Length:	8.6 km (5.4 mi.) allow 3 to 4 hrs. one way
Difficulty Level:	Moderately difficult. Short difficult section beyond tunnel.

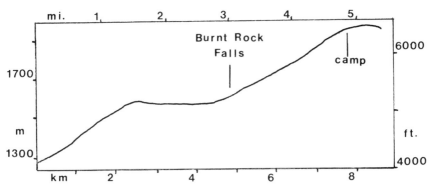

ACCESS Crypt Lake Trail begins at Crypt Landing on the east side of Upper Waterton Lake. Charter boat service from Waterton townsite is used to reach the landing and return. Check with the Information Centre for schedules and rates or inquire at the marina. Access overland to Crypt Lake Trail is via Vimy Peak (47) and Bosporus (48) trails. **HORSES:** Use the overland access as above or the Dardanelles river crossing -- see Vimy Peak Trail (47).

ATTRACTIONS Crypt Landing, an attractive camping and picnicing spot with beach, boat dock and horse corral. Several major waterfalls along trail. Travel through natural tunnel. Beautiful lake backed by massive headwall. Lake has large cutthroat trout. Alpine flowers in Crypt Basin, including the rare pygmy poppy, *Papaver pygmaeum*. Basin is home to grey-crowned rosy finch and mountain goats.

CONSIDERATIONS Return boat arrangements across Waterton Lake should be made before you leave; be sure to allow plenty of time on the hike out to catch your boat. Crypt is a high country trail; carry warm clothing even on sunny days. Snow may persist into midsummer here; check with the Information Centre for trail conditions. Shortcutting on switch back is causing serious erosion on this delicate mountain terrain; **please stay on the trail.** Much of the trail is a long uphill grade on open mountainside and can be quite hot; plan an early start and carry water. For access to Crypt Lake basin, hikers must crawl through a 25-metre tunnel and there is considerable vertical exposure for a short distance beyond, although there are cable assists. Return by same route. There is no camping at Crypt Lake; Crypt Lake campsite is located below Crypt basin before the tunnel. **HORSES:** It is not possible to ride beyond Crypt Lake campsite; riders must proceed to Crypt basin on foot. The Hell Roaring Falls spur is not recommended for horses.

THE TRAIL Crypt Landing is a beautiful starting point for the journey to Crypt Lake. Whether you are hiking, boating or riding, this small cove with its peaceful beach surrounded by fir and spruce forest is an ideal setting. Camp for the night or spend an afternoon on shore with a side trip to Hell Roaring Falls. The short spur to these falls branches off ½ km along the main trail and travels 1 km to a rocky promontory overlooking Hell Roaring Gorge. In spring and early summer a torrent of turquoise water swirls through red and copper-colored rock. Hikers continuing to Crypt Lake can connect with the main trail by following a poorly-defined steep path beyond the falls.

The main trail ascends a cool, shaded ridge through heavy spruce and fir forest with varied underbrush, including delicious thimbleberries in late July. This steep climb is eased by a series of switchbacks; please stay on the trail and avoid further eroding of the thin mountain soil. Twin Falls enhances this part of the trip and an overlook there offers a good resting place. The trail levels as it continues up Hell Roaring Valley along the south-facing slope of Vimy Peak to Burnt Rock Falls. The rusty iron oxide of the hard dolomitic limestone it tumbles over gives Burnt Rock Falls its name. Here, older limestone rests atop younger red Grinnell argillite, a result of the Crandell thrust movement. The fault fracture is visible at the base of the falls.

As the trail rises above the valley floor, it begins a series of steep switchbacks across an open slope of rock and shale. A strenuous hike, this section is often very hot in summer sun. Riders may wish to lead their horses up this section. High on the traverse a fine view surrounds you from Crypt Falls at the head of the steep-walled valley to a marshy lake far below. At 7.9 km the trail levels in a shady stand of alpine fir beside a refreshing stream. Here, Crypt Lake campsite marks the end of the trail for horses and a hitch rail is provided. After crossing the creek just beyond the campsite, you begin the final .8 km to Crypt Lake basin. Hoary marmots may whistle as you pass through their bouldery home to Crypt Tunnel. This natural opening through a massive limestone abutment is the passageway to the beauty of Crypt Basin. Though the tunnel has been enlarged, hikers still have to crawl through it mid-section and considerable vertical exposure occurs as soon as you emerge. Anchored steel cables assist hikers as the trail climbs a short distance up a rock precipice. Move slowly and concentrate on your footing along this section. The trail passes through a subalpine forest and levels again alongside a limestone ledge that has been eroded into terraces and is covered with a mossy alpine garden. The underground outlet from Crypt Lake emerges from a cave in this ledge and tumbles 175 metres to form Crypt Falls. It is a few more upward steps to Crypt Basin.

Crypt Lake, which touches the International Boundary at its southern tip, is surrounded on three sides by high walls. Mountain goats are commonly seen, as is the grey-crowned rosy finch. Snowfields remain throughout the year and icebergs often float in the lake until late summer. Frigid waters provide excellent trout habitat and the cutthroat grow large, but are tantalizingly hard to catch in the clear water. Long summer days tempt you to linger, enjoying the basin, but be sure to allow at least three hours for the hike to your boat at Crypt Landing.

Crypt Lake Tunnel.

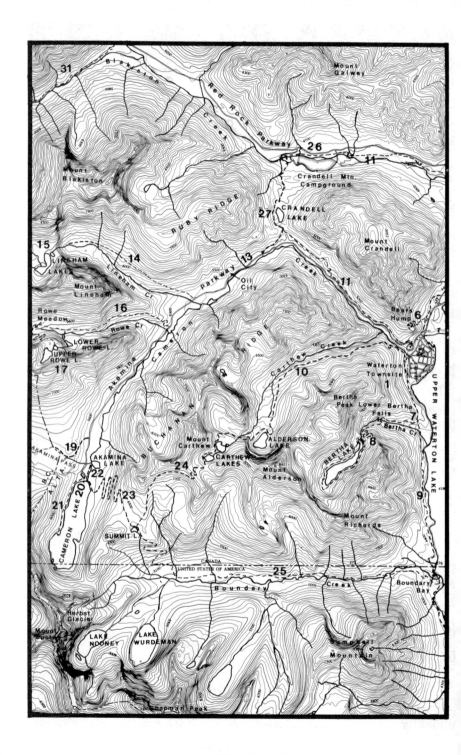

AKAMINA PARKWAY

40

13 AKAMINA PARKWAY

TRAILHEAD FOR:
Crandell Lake (27), Lineham Creek (14), Lineham Lakes Basin Route (15), Rowe Meadow (16), Upper Rowe (17), Tamarack (18), Akamina Pass Trail and B.C. destinations (19) and Cameron Lake (20).

Akamina Parkway leaves Waterton Valley between the Information Bureau and Emerald Bay, and winds 16 km (10 mi.) up Cameron Creek Valley between high mountains. Viewpoints along the first part of the roadway offer striking views of Waterton Valley and down into Cameron Creek gorge. Gradually the Parkway converges with Cameron Creek and there are several pleasant places to stop. Formal picnic sites are at McNealy's (6.4 km) and Little Prairie (13.3 km), but there are many other places to enjoy the valley forests and running water. Unmarked paths lead along the edge of the stream to gentle waterfalls and good trout pools where you can fish from Victoria Day to Labor Day. As you drive along the Parkway, the mountain slopes and valleys along the road offer a glimpse of what the trails from this access route have to offer.

An informative radio broadcast about this area is provided by the Park's interpretive service from June through September. Watch signs along the Parkway for dial settings. The site of Western Canada's first producing oil well is located at 8.1 km; a roadside exhibit and a pamphlet called *Oil City*, available on-site and at the Information Bureau, gives interesting historical background on this discovery and its development. Another plaque and a short path at 9.3 km marks the former Oil City townsite.

During the winter months, this Parkway may be open to Little Prairie picnic site for Nordic skiing to Cameron Lake and Akamina Pass. However, the road is subject to avalanches and may be closed. Check with the Park Administration or phone 859-2445 for winter conditions.

14 LINEHAM CREEK

Trailhead:	Akamina Parkway
Destination:	Viewpoint for Lineham Falls, base of Lineham Cliff
Length:	4.2 km (2.6 mi.) allow 1 to 2 hrs. one way
Difficulty Level:	Moderately easy

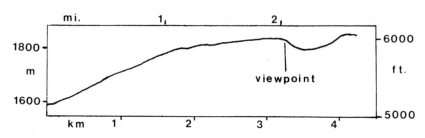

ACCESS The trail begins at an unmarked pullout 9.3 km (5.8 mi.) along the Akamina Parkway (13). It is on the right-hand side just before the Oil City townsite plaque.

ATTRACTIONS Lineham Falls cascading more than 100 metres to the bottom of Lineham Cliff. Wildflowers. A close-up look at Mount Lineham.

CONSIDERATIONS Trail crosses an open hillside and can be very hot and dry. No water before second half of trail. Return by same route. No facilities.

THE TRAIL If you are intrigued by high cliffs and waterfalls, you will enjoy this trail. As you leave the pine forest of Cameron Valley, the path rises quickly and breaks into the open along a steep grassy hillside, a wintering area for bighorn sheep. The thirst you'll work up along this waterless stretch can be quenched by the trickling streams and cool shade that await ahead as the trail levels out and re-enters a coniferous forest. As the trees thin, you emerge to a dramatic view. Mount Lineham towers to your left, Mount Blakiston to the right; together they frame the sheer face of Lineham Cliff with its slender waterfall sliding down from the hanging basin above. The trail continues up the valley and alongside a large deposit of Purcell lava boulders; their origin is an on-going topic for geologists. The trail ends near the base of the cliff. Sit for awhile, have a snack and glass the rock walls with your binoculars for white mountain goat and bighorn sheep.

15 LINEHAM LAKES BASIN ROUTE

Trailhead: Akamina Parkway
Destination: Lineham Lakes Basin
Length: 5.6 km (3.5 mi.) allow 2½ to 3 hrs. one way
Difficulty Level: Difficult (Hazardous Activity)

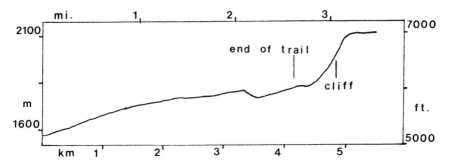

ACCESS The Lineham Lakes Basin Route continues from the Lineham Creek Trail (14).

ATTRACTIONS Glacier-carved hanging valley, the Lineham Lakes alpine basin. Lineham Cliff. Fishing for cutthroat trout.

CONSIDERATIONS Routes into Lineham Basin are not Park trails and are neither maintained nor defined. Access requires a traverse across a 100-metre high, sheer cliff and the vertical exposure is extreme. The traverse is considered a hazardous activity and hikers should obtain a Registration for a Hazardous Activity from a Park warden. This ascent should only be attempted by experienced climbers with no fear of heights. Do not attempt the traverse in foul or threatening weather; routes are especially dangerous in wet weather or fog. Return by same route. Lineham Basin camping, for which a backcountry camping permit is required, is undesignated and no open fires are allowed.

THE TRAIL Lineham Cliff stands as a sentry to the beauty of Lineham Lakes Basin. The sheer precipice of Lineham Cliff must first be traversed to gain entrance to this remote hanging valley. Two routes, one on each side of the cascading waterfall, feel their way across the rock face. Climbers may come face-to-face with mountain goats as these routes are actually game trails; sheep and goats often use them to travel in and out of the basin.

From the top of the cliff, the beauty of Lineham Basin waits to be explored. A series of low ridges run across the valley floor and ancient forests of alpine larch, limber pine and spruce conceal the lakes, streams and gentle waterfalls that adorn the basin. Two of Lineham's five lakes offer good trout fishing. The day passes quickly in this high country; be sure to leave plenty of daylight and energy for the trip back across the cliff. If you are camping, remember that this alpine meadow is delicate. Choose your campsite carefully and disturb as little as possible. Please pack out all that you pack in.

16 ROWE MEADOW

Trailhead: Akamina Parkway
Destination: Rowe Meadow
Length: 5.2 km (3.2 mi.) allow 2 to 3 hrs. one way
Difficulty Level: Moderately easy

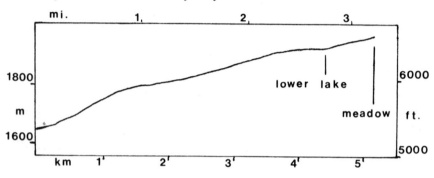

ACCESS Trail begins at the Rowe Lakes automobile pullout 10.7 km (6.6 mi.) up the Akamina Parkway from the town-site.

ATTRACTIONS Easy access to alpine meadow. Wildflowers. Lower Rowe Lake. **HORSES:** Wide trail with moderate grade provides good conditioning ride for horses unaccustomed to mountain terrain.

CONSIDERATIONS Poor fishing in Lower Rowe Lake. Return by same route.

THE TRAIL The streams of Waterton Park are considered by many to be among the most beautiful in the Rockies. Rowe Creek is no exception. The lower trail follows alongside the creek which cascades through a chute of red argillite. The combination of motion and color give the trail a lovely beginning. As the trail climbs, it leaves the semi-open creekside and moves in under the cool canopy of a mature forest. The combination of open area and protected shade that characterizes this trail provides a variety of flowers. Indian paintbrush in a dozen shades thrive in the summer as do the creamy mariposa lily, yellow columbine and brilliant blue beard tongue. The forest understory hosts the white queen's cup and the foam flower.

At 3.9 km, a short spur trail leads left to Lower Rowe Lake. Set against an impressive 150-metre cliff, the lake is inhabited by small Eastern brook trout and is a pleasant final destination if you've had enough climbing. The main trail continues up about 1 km to Rowe Meadow, a beautiful amphitheatre surrounded on three sides by high mountains. A cool stream wandering through the grassy green offers a fine setting for picnicing. Alpine flowers are even more plentiful here as the species along the lower trail are joined by monkey flower, arnica and beargrass according to the season.

For strong hikers Rowe Meadow Junction offers two opportunities. The Upper Rowe Trail (17) continues on a short, but steep, climb to a hanging valley holding the upper lakes; and the demanding Tamarack Trail (18) climbs out of the basin on its long journey into Waterton's western regions.

17 UPPER ROWE LAKES

Trailhead: Rowe Meadow
Destination: Upper Rowe Lakes
Length: 6.3 km (3.9 mi.) allow 2½ to 3 hrs. one way
Difficulty Level: Moderately difficult

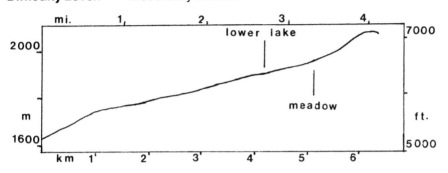

ACCESS   Upper Rowe Lakes Trail is a continuation of the Rowe Meadow Trail (16) from Akamina Parkway.

ATTRACTIONS   Relatively easy access to a hanging valley. Beautiful hike in the fall though alpine larch forest.

CONSIDERATIONS   The trail is steep. No fish. Return by same route.

THE TRAIL   The trail to Upper Rowe branches left at the trail junction just above Rowe Meadow and begins a steep climb to the hanging valley. Switchbacks make this climb a little easier. In the fall, asters and fireweed complement the golden alpine larch that line the trail. This and other hanging valleys in the Park, such as Lineham and Bertha, were formed by glacial action. A small glacier high on the mountainside gradually gouged out this basin. At the same time a much larger glacier was carving a deeper valley which now contains Rowe Meadow. When the ice melted this small cirque was left hanging above the main valley.

Middle Rowe Lake is the first of the two lakes you see. At high water it spills over the lip of the valley, cascading 150 metres to Lower Rowe Lake. In drier times, it merely seeps through the porous limestone. Upper Rowe Lake is relatively large, but quite shallow. The high rock ridges surrounding the basin form part of the Continental Divide. You may see bighorn sheep on the slopes as you wander around this peaceful high country, and if you are fortunate and listen carefully, you may also hear the clash of horns as two rams joust.

The alpine larches, which are common in this high basin, are noted for both their soft summer green and fall gold. They are the last trees of any size to grow near the timberline and this genus includes the only Waterton conifer to lose its needles in the fall.

18 TAMARACK

Trailhead: Rowe Meadow
Destination: Lone Lake
Length: For above distance only: 12.7 km (7.9 mi.) allow 6 to hrs. Combined distance including necessary access trails: 31.6 km (19.6 mi.) 2 full days
Difficulty Level: Moderately difficult

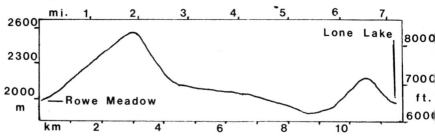

ACCESS The Tamarack Trail may be travelled from two directions. From the Akamina Parkway (13) travel the Rowe Meadow Trail (16) to its junction with the Tamarack Trail. From Red Rock Canyon (28) travel the Lone Lake Trail (41) south from Blakiston Junction.

ATTRACTIONS An extended tour of Waterton's varied terrain, flora and fauna. Extraordinary view from Lineham Ridge. Travel into Waterton's remote backcountry. Highest trail summit in the Park at 2560 metres.

CONSIDERATIONS The actual Tamarack trail extends 12.7 km from Rowe Meadow to Lone Lake. However, to travel the Tamarack, a number of trails must be negotiated and the combined distance is 31.6 km (19.6 mi.) requiring at least two full days of travel. (This combined route is often referred to as the Tamarack Trail. For clarity, it is here called the Tamarack Tour.) This is a strenuous hike, allow lots of time. Water is scarce, carry some and check the Park topographical map for sources before departing. Major sections above treeline offer no protection from wind or bad weather and travellers are especially vulnera-

ble to hypothermia. (Please see Hypothermia in the introductory section.) Most of the trail is well-marked, but becomes difficult and dangerous in fog and cloudy conditions. The complete tour requires overnighting; camping facilities are at Lone Lake and Twin Lakes.

HORSES: The trail travels high mountain terrain; horses must be well-conditioned and accustomed to alpine travel. A steep chute must be negotiated on the final summit ascent and horses have to be led. Carry adequate feed as no grazing is permitted. Horse camping at Lone Lake and Snowshoe Cabin (by permission).

THE TRAIL Although named for the stands of alpine larch (tamarack) that line parts of the trail, much of the Tamarack travels open scree slopes high above the treeline. From the Akamina Parkway, the Tamarack Tour travels 5.2 km to Rowe Meadow. Hikers and riders may wish to rest in the meadow and fill up with water for the demanding climb ahead. The Tamarack Trail branches right just beyond the meadow and in one long sweeping arc quickly rises above the green basin as it traverses the open scree slope at the head of Rowe Valley. Switchbacks high

46

above the treeline help you reach a shoulder of Lineham ridge. Rock cairns and orange trail markers distinguish the route from game trails that crisscross this open slope. The trail continues to reach for the summit as it climbs the ridge separating Rowe and Lineham valleys. A steep chute must be negotiated on the final summit ascent.

The view from this elevated world is breathtaking. A panorama of mountain peaks and lakes extends in every direction. The expanse of the mountain world is a contrast to the micro-world at your feet as hardy alpine plants cling to the colorful rocks with tentacled roots. From the summit, the trail slopes down to a saddle above Lineham Basin, offering a good vantage point for seeing the chain of lakes there. Rest your legs and your horses here; the descent from this high place is as demanding as the journey up. Careful attention to your footing is required on the steep talus slope as the trail switchbacks down 730

metres. The alpine meadow below offers a perfect rest stop and water is available below the trail to the east. (Those approaching from Lone Lake should rest here before making the demanding climb up and over to Rowe Basin.)

The trail continues north, closely paralleling the headwall that forms the Continental Divide, to a second steep climb over a shoulder of Festubert Mountain. From the shoulder, a quick downhill section connects with the Lone Lake Trail (41) at the backcountry facilities adjacent to Lone Lake. To complete the tour in this direction proceed to Blakiston Junction along the Lone Lake Trail (42 km) and then to Red Rock Canyon via either of two routes. The shorter, downhill all-the-way route is via Blakiston Valley Trail (31) (10.1 km). The longer route (14.7 km) travels the Blue Grouse Basin (40) to Twin Lakes (38) and east to Red Rock Canyon along the Snowshoe Trail (33).

19 AKAMINA PASS

Trailhead: Akamina Parkway
Destination: Akamina Pass, the Park boundary with British Columbia, access to Wall Lake, B.C. and Akamina Valley, B.C.
Length: 1.6 km (1 mi.) to Park Boundary; allow 1 hr. one way. 5.6 (3.5 mi.) to Wall Lake from Parkway; 2 to 3 hrs. one way.
Difficulty Level: Moderately easy

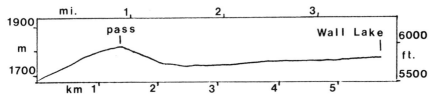

ACCESS   A roadside sign at the pullout ⅛ km (½ mi.) before Cameron Lake parking lot indicates the trailhead for Akamina Pass.

ATTRACTIONS   A wooded walk up to the Continental Divide and the Alberta-

B.C. border. Approach to Wall Lake and B.C.'s Akamina Valley.

CONSIDERATIONS   Not a view trail. Return by same path. B.C. fishing license required for Wall Lake fishing.

THE TRAIL   Originally a wagon road, the Akamina Pass Trail was used during the early days of this century for oil exploration. The heavily-forested trail leads to a low (1600 metre) pass over the Continental Divide which also marks the boundary between Waterton Park and British Columbia.

Akamina Pass is also a popular Nordic ski route; the downhill grade from the top of the pass provides a challenging run. However, winter access may be limited. Check with the Park Administration for winter conditions.

B.C. DESTINATIONS

WALL LAKE and FORUM LAKE, B.C.   Trails in the area beyond Akamina Pass are maintained by B.C. Parks. Trails are gradually being developed in this recently-designated recreational area. There is a seasonal Parks Headquarters about 500 metres beyond the Waterton boundary. About 400 metres along the main trail from the top of the pass, the 100 metre trail to the headquarters cabins branches left (south). The 1.5 km trail to Forum Lake proceeds south from the headquarters. Forum Lake has no outlet, but there are springs along the trail below the lake. Above the lake, on the left, is a fine example of a pure larch forest.

Beyond this first turnoff a second trail branches left from the main trail and leads to Wall Lake. This lake is a popular destination and attracts many people who like to fish for the native cutthroat trout during the season. A British Columbia fishing license can be obtained from the Waterton Park Information Centre. The trail circles the lake and there are a couple of camping areas. One, near a lagoon on the west side of the lake, is particularly pleasant. The spectacular headwall that gives the lake its name clearly reveals several layers of the sedimentary rock that forms these mountains. A mineral lick and treed ledges attract goats to the cliff at times.

Routes continue on into the Akamina Valley as well as up on to Akamina Ridge which lies to the south of both Forum and Wall lakes. Routes beyond Wall and Forum on Akamina Ridge should only be travelled in fair weather. See **CONSIDERATIONS** for Carthew-Alderson (24). These routes also continue west into the Kintla Valley. The route into the Akamina Valley (a continuation of the main trail) travels through clear-cut patches. In the late seventies and early eighties a cyclic infestation of pine bark beetle killed many large stands of lodgepole pine in southern B.C. and Alberta. In Waterton Lakes National Park, this natural process was allowed to take its course, but outside the park salvage logging was carried out and the route may be hard to follow. Travellers beyond Wall and Forum lakes should purchase the Sage Creek quadrangle map 82 G/1 for this area.

Boundary Creek and Lake Wurdeman.

Carthew Lakes Basin.

20 CAMERON LAKE

TRAILHEAD FOR:
Cameron Lakeshore (21), Akamina Lake (22), Summit Lake (23), Carthew-Alderson (24) and Boundary Creek (25) trails.

Cameron Lake, the terminus of the Akamina Parkway, offers a scenic introduction to this unique area. Stepping out of your car, you enter a subalpine setting of a cool lake, dark forest, and snowy mountains; a tantalizing introduction that whets the appetite for exploring the trails accessible from this point.

Carved from the mountains that form the Continental Divide, Cameron Lake is situated on Waterton's southwest border. To the south, Mount Custer marks the border between Canada and the United States, and the ridge running north from Forum Peak is the border with British Columbia. The combination of high elevation and moist air flowing over the mountains from the Pacific creates heavy precipitation, usually in the form of snow which persists here for six to eight months of the year. Snow covers the top of Mount Custer most of the time. All this moisture produces a particularly heavy, dark green subalpine forest. An interpretive exhibit housed at Cameron Lake tells the story of the surrounding landscape: its geology, forests and inhabitants.

A popular family recreation area, Cameron Lake provides a variety of activities and facilities. Canoes, paddle boats and row boats can be rented at the lake or you can launch your own boat (no motors) to get a closer look at Mount Custer. Boats also offer a good, safe way to observe grizzly bears that are sometimes visible on the avalanche slopes at the far end of the lake. Cameron Lake attracts anglers for the season from Victoria Day through Labor Day and offers both boat fishing and good shoreline angling. Well-placed picnic sites together with an easy stroll along the lakeshore makes Cameron an ideal day's destination.

21 CAMERON LAKESHORE TRAIL

Trailhead:	Cameron Lake
Destination:	Trail ends on the lakeshore at the edge of the avalanche slope below Mount Custer.
Length:	1.6 km (1 mi.) allow ½ to 1 hr. one way
Difficulty Level:	Easy

ACCESS The trail begins at the parking lot and proceeds along the west shore of Cameron Lake.

ATTRACTIONS An easy lakeshore stroll. Views of Mount Custer. Lakeshore fishing. Likely area for wildlife; bring your binoculars.

CONSIDERATIONS The trail does

not circle the lake. Do **not** go beyond the end of the trail as the avalanche slope has a high incidence of grizzly bear activity. No facilities along the trail. Return by same trail.

THE TRAIL The easy level path along a beautiful mountain lakeshore makes this one of the Park's most popular trails. A walk through dark green forests of Engleman spruce and subalpine fir is highlighted by views of the slopes of Mount Custer which flanks the southern end of the lake.

There is good shoreline fishing from Victoria Day to Labor Day. Small colorful patches of wildflowers, including monkey flower and grass-of-parnassus, bloom in seepage spots along the trail while the woods shelter subalpine birds such as the song sparrow, Wilson's warbler, grey jay, and both species of crossbill. The open, brushy avalanche slope beyond the trail's end is one of the most likely places in the Park to observe a grizzly bear. Deer and black bears also browse the mountainside.

22 AKAMINA LAKE

Trailhead:	Cameron Lake
Destination:	Akamina Lake
Length:	.5 km (.3 mi.) allow 15 min. one way
Difficulty Level:	Easy

ACCESS At Cameron Lake, the trail starts on the east side of the parking lot or at the orientation signs. Akamina Lake may also be reached by a trail from the automobile pullout on the left side of the Akamina Parkway just before the Cameron Lake parking lot.

ATTRACTIONS The Cameron Lake access is popular with fisherman. Marshy habitat, good for moose. Good birding path.

CONSIDERATIONS Area around Akamina Lake is often muddy; flies and mosquitoes may be numerous. Access path from automobile pullout is not regularly maintained. Return by same route.

THE TRAIL Originally a fishermen's footpath, the trail from Cameron Lake meanders through marshy evergreen forest along Cameron Creek as it flows through Akamina Lake on its way to Waterton Valley. This clear sparkling stream provides excellent spawning grounds for rainbow and brook trout from Cameron Lake. Moose prefer the small, shallow, boggy Akamina Lake and such birds as the deep blue Steller's jay, the ruby-crowned kinglet and the varied thrush nest in the trees here. In spring, yellow violets bloom profusely in the damp ground and there may be mushrooms in the fall.

23 SUMMIT LAKE

Trailhead: Cameron Lake
Destination: Summit Lake
Length: 4 km (2.5 mi.) allow 1½ to 2 hrs. one way
Difficulty Level: Moderately difficult

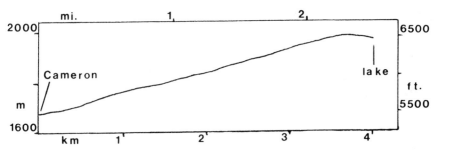

ACCESS From the Cameron Creek footbridge, the Summit Lake Trail initially heads south, paralleling the east shore of Cameron Lake (20).

ATTRACTIONS Views above Cameron Lake include Herbst Glacier on Mount Custer, and Forum Peak which marks the boundary between Alberta and British Columbia in Canada and Montana in the United States.

CONSIDERATIONS Steep uphill grade. No facilities. Trail may be wet and boggy in early summer. Return by same route.

THE TRAIL This hike takes you through a wet subalpine forest unique in Waterton.

The trail climbs 250 metres in a series of switchbacks through 300-year-old spruce and fir trees. As you near the crest, Cameron Lake is spread out below and your view extends over the Continental Divide into British Columbia's Akamina Valley. The trail tops the ridge and the dense subalpine forest gives way to well-spaced whitebark pines and alpine larch. Blown-down trees expose their large root pans and reveal the thin soil here. Summit Lake sits on a small plateau and reflects Montana's Chapman Peak with the Wurdeman Glacier on its slopes. The lake, once known as "Mother Duck", is often a nesting site for a family of Barrow's Goldeneye. The Carthew-Alderson (24) and Boundary Creek (25) trails continue from here. Unless you are equipped for a long hike and the weather is promising, you should return to Cameron Lake.

24 CARTHEW-ALDERSON

Trailhead:	Cameron Lake
Destination:	Waterton Townsite
Length:	19 km (12 mi.) allow 6 to 8 hrs. one way
Difficulty Level:	Moderately difficult

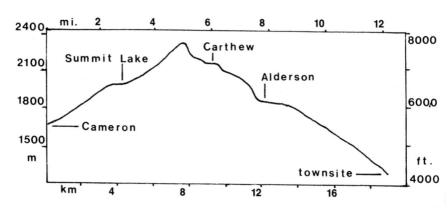

ACCESS Carthew-Alderson is accessible from either end of Cameron Valley. The journey can begin at Cameron Lake via Summit Lake Trail (23) or in Waterton townsite at Cameron Falls via Alderson Lake Trail (10). The Cameron Lake approach is the most popular with hikers as it eliminates 500 metres of uphill hiking.

ATTRACTIONS Spectacular trail in good weather with superb high mountain views. Offers a cross-sectional study of Waterton's terrain and vegetation. Good fishing at Lower Carthew and Alderson lakes. Backcountry camping facilities and horse corrals at Alderson Lake.

CONSIDERATIONS This is a fair-weather hike. Carthew Summit is subject to extreme and fast-changing weather conditions; rain, fog, snow, lightning and cold temperatures are likely at any time. Wind velocities can be extreme. The terrain at the summit is exposed to these elements and offers no protection. At these elevations, hikers and riders are especially susceptible to hypothermia. Take extra clothing such as toque, gloves, sweater and rain gear, **even on sunny days.** The trail across the summit may be difficult or impossible to follow in fog or snow; turn back if you ascend into inclement weather. Game trails near the summit can be confused with the main trail; watch carefully for orange trail markers. There is no water between Summit Lake and Upper Carthew and much of this section is on bare, rocky scree slopes that can be hot and dry. No facilities exist between Cameron and Alderson Lakes. Transportation must be arranged to or from Cameron Lake trailhead. **HORSES:** Hazardous snowfields may persist until late summer. Check with Information Bureau about conditions. Hazardous rock makes travel around Lower Carthew dangerous. Ride horses in the lake, staying close to the shoreline. Move slowly as rocky bottom provides difficult footing. Leaving Carthew Basin, the trail drops over a steep rock ledge. Riders should check cinches here and lead their mounts down this short section.

THE TRAIL The Carthew-Alderson Trail connects Cameron Lake with Waterton Townsite. Its length, covering a variety of terrain, and its height, giving wide-angle views, make it one of Waterton's most spectacular trails. From Cameron Lake follow the Summit Lake Trail to the Summit Lake Junction. There a sign directs you to the left and north along the Carthew-Alderson Trail. Climbing quickly from the lake, the trail travels through stunted, twisted sub-alpine fir and whitebark pine. These are the survivors on a slope often ravaged by winter avalanches sliding from Mount Carthew into the alpine meadow below. As the trail curves around the south face of the ridge, the view into remote northern Glacier Park unfolds. Nooney and Wurdeman Lakes closely clutched in their steep-walled basins contrast their icy blue-green with the soft yellow-green of the nearer meadow. Distant glaciers hang on the steep rock faces above these lakes.

Rising above the treeline the trail switchbacks across red argillite scree slopes toward the summit. Travel beyond treeline is a special experience and one that rewards a sense of observation. No trees interrupt your view here, but the vegetation is remarkable. Alpine plants such as moss campion, mountain dryas, sky pilot and silky phacelia cling to the thin soil protected from the powerful winds that roar across this summit by fractured shale slabs. Their bright pinks and yellows, dusty greens and blues contrast with the red of argillite scree. This red rock is of the Kintla formation and is one of many layers of sedimentary rock that compose these mountains. Each layer reveals different characteristics of structure and color. A pause at the Carthew Ridge summit reveals a truly splendid view. You can see still further into Glacier Park and the view into Carthew Lakes extends out across the Alberta prairies. An unmarked side route to the right leads to a rock prominence overlooking Boundary Creek valley.

From the summit, follow the orange markers as the trail descends quickly down the north slope into Carthew Lakes basin. Snow persists here year-round and care should be taken when crossing drifts. Move slowly and place your feet firmly; a walking stick helps. The subalpine world that appears as you descend into Upper Carthew basin reflects its elevated environment. Winter avalanches determine placement of vegetation here. Although they may be hundreds of years older, the trees are stunted and spreading in contrast to the tall, straight conifers of the subalpine forest along the Summit Lake Trail.

Upper Carthew Lake spills into the lower lake over a lip of Purcell lava draped with carpets of alpine flowers and mosses. As you descend alongside the gentle falls, you may see the ripples of rising cutthroat in the lake below. The trail continues around the lake to the left and passes over a slanted rock outcropping. Leaving Carthew basin, the trail travels through windswept fir trees (*krumholtz*) before dropping over a rock rim of the Siyeh formation, another sedimentary layer, via a series of short switchbacks.

The turquoise of Alderson Lake, set against one of the highest sheer cliffs in Waterton, provides yet another of the magnificent views that distinguish this trail. Camping facilities and trout fishing at Alderson Lake provide a perfect place to spend the night. From here it is a steady downhill descent that takes several hours to Waterton townsite, as described in Alderson Lake Trail (10).

25 BOUNDARY CREEK

Trailhead: Summit Lake
Destination: Boundary Bay
Length: 13.4 km (8.3 mi.) to Boundary Bay; allow 3 hrs. one w.
Difficulty Level: Moderately easy from Summit Lake. Moderately difficu if hiked in reverse from Boundary Bay.

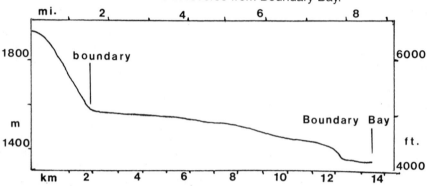

ACCESS Boundary Creek Trail is most often approached along the Summit Lake Trail (23). At Summit Lake it proceeds straight ahead along the shore of the lake. The trail may also be hiked in reverse. It joins the Lakeshore Trail (9) .5 km beyond Boundary Bay, just south of Boundary Creek.

ATTRACTIONS Travel into a remote part of Waterton Park along the International Boundary with Montana's Glacier National Park.

CONSIDERATIONS Remote trail, seldom travelled. Bears feed in bountiful huckleberry patches along the trail. Be careful! No facilities between Cameron Lake and Boundary Bay. If hiked from Boundary Bay, the ascent to Summit Lake is a steep, demanding climb. Be sure to compute access trail distances when planning this hike. **HORSES:** Creek crossings are rocky and fast running water or driftwood may be a problem. Watch for safe fords. The trail through the valley bottom is eroded in places. Exposed roots may make footing difficult.

THE TRAIL This trail parallels the southern boundary of Waterton and crosses the International Border into Glacier National Park for most of its length. From the shore of Summit Lake, the trail descends a high ridge. Views into Glacier Park's Nooney and Wurdeman Lakes are unforgettable. The route switchbacks through large huckleberry patches as it drops 412 metres (1350 ft.) into the heavily-forested Boundary Creek Valley.

As you travel the north side of the valley, the stream alongside carves its way through deep red and cool green argillite in a series of waterfalls until it reaches Boundary Bay on Waterton Lake. The trail meets the Lakeshore Trail (9) in Glacier Park .5 km south of the International Boundary. From here you can travel north along the Lakeshore Trail back to Waterton townsite (6.3 km) or south 6.7 km to Goat Haunt Ranger Station where tour boats can provide transportation back to Waterton townsite. Check with the Information Bureau before leaving for schedules and fares.

26 RED ROCK PARKWAY

TRAILHEAD FOR:
Crandell Lake Trail (27), and access to Crandell Campground, Canyon Camp and Red Rock Canyon Trailhead (28).

Red Rock Parkway branches off the Park entrance road 2 km (1.2 mi.) north of the Information Bureau and proceeds 14 km (8.75 mi.) to Red Rock Canyon. A roadside sign and the bridge across Blakiston Creek mark the turnoff.

A drive along Red Rock Parkway is an introduction to Waterton's distinctive "where the mountains meet the prairies" terrain. As the road crosses the southern edge of the Alberta prairie, the treeless grassy plain seems to run right up the side of Bellevue Hill. This combination of prairie and mountain habitat makes Waterton Park rich in wildlife as species from both habitats exist in close proximity. Elk, deer and bighorn sheep are often visible along this winding highway and the lucky visitor may even glimpse a cougar (mountain lion) on the rock ledges above the road. Once, huge herds of plains bison (buffalo) also roamed this area and Indians used the steep stream bank along Blakiston Creek as a buffalo jump for harvesting these animals. Today, an interpretive display at 4.9 km provides an interesting account of this technique.

Travelling up the Parkway, you are treated to views of craggy Mount Galwey on the right; Waterton's highest peak, 2942-metre Mount Blakiston on the left; and Mount Anderson ahead.

Mountain passes at the head of this valley were heavily used by Indians and explorers and the stream here is still known locally as Pass Creek. Modern explorers can learn more about this valley as they drive along by tuning to an interpretive radio broadcast. Watch roadside signs for dial settings. Interpretive plaques at pullouts along the way and pleasant picnic sites at Coppermine Creek (9.3 km) and Lost Horse Creek (11.5 km) welcome visitors. Crandell Campground (6.6 km) and Canyon Camp (7.8 km) are also located here.

27 CRANDELL LAKE

Trailhead:	Red Rock Parkway. Akamina Parkway	
Destination:	Crandell Lake	
Length:	2.0 km (1.2 mi.) from Crandell Campground; allow 1 hr one way. 1.2 km (0.7 mi.) from Akamina Parkway; allow 1/2 to 3/4 hr. one way	
Difficulty Level:	Moderately easy	

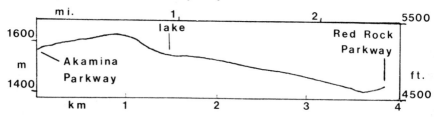

ACCESS Crandell Lake is located in a connecting basin that runs from the Red Rock Parkway (26) to the Akamina Parkway (13) and may be approached from either. From Red Rock Parkway, Crandell Campground campers should use the path that leaves the southwest corner of the campground and joins the Crandell Lake Trail beyond the Canyon Camp. Hikers and riders arriving by vehicle should park in the grassy parking lot 0.4 km along the Canyon Camp entrance road, walk across the bridge and a sign will direct you to the trail. From the Akamina Parkway, a sign 7 km from Waterton townsite marks the trailhead.

ATTRACTIONS Good family stroll. Wide, graded trail well-suited for group hikes. Sheltered on windy days. Scenic picnic area and sandy beach at Crandell Lake. Nordic ski route with access from Akamina Parkway, though not maintained. Cycling permitted.

CONSIDERATIONS This is a heavily-used trail; please help to maintain the beauty of the area by staying on the designated trails and keeping picnic areas clean.

The Crandell Campground access is for campers only. Others please use vehicle access described above. **HORSES:** Riders, do not travel in or through the Crandell campgrounds. **CYCLISTS:** This trail is heavily used. Please travel slowly and cautiously.

THE TRAIL A million years ago, the great Cameron glaciers gouged their way through the mountains here to form this small basin connecting with the Blakiston valley. Early travellers soon recognized the convenience of this natural passageway between Waterton's two main valleys, and today's trail follows the old wagon road that was used at the turn of the century for access to oil discovery sites in Cameron Valley. From the Red Rock Parkway, this short easy trail climbs a series of rocky benches through shady trees to Crandell Lake. A sheltered path, it is lined with wildflowers during June and July. Picnic and camping spots at the lake and good fishing make this a popular family trail. From the Akamina Parkway, it is an easy stroll to the lake. On the return trip, there is a short uphill grade as the trail climbs a small ridge before sloping back down to the Parkway.

Interpretive hikes are offered by both Waterton and Glacier Park Intepreters.

Feldspar Phenocryst rock formation.

Bear Grass, *Xerophyllum tenax.*

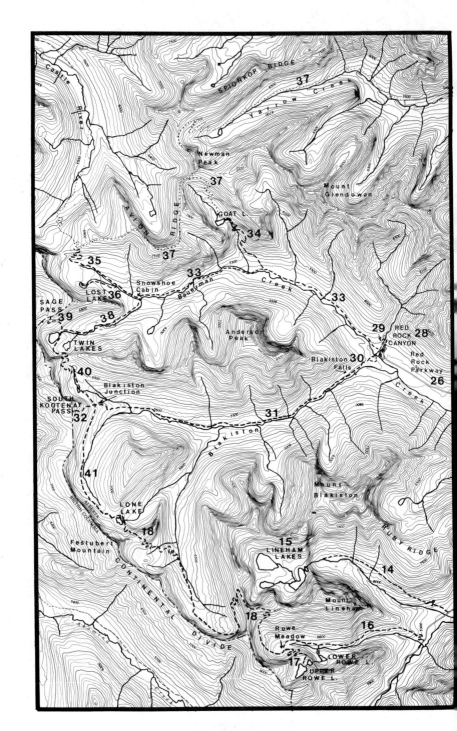

NORTH WEST REGION

28 RED ROCK CANYON

TRAILHEAD FOR:
Red Rock Canyon Loop (29), Blakiston Falls (30), Blakiston Valley (31), South Kootenay Pass (32), Snowshoe (33), Goat Lake (34), Lost Lake (36), Castle River Divide (35), Avion Ridge Route (37), Twin Lakes (38), Sage Pass (39), Blue Grouse Basin(40), Lone Lake (41), and Tamarack Trail (18).

Red Rock Canyon is the terminus of Red Rock Parkway (26) 14 km (8.75 mi.) from the junction with the Park entrance road. Throughout the year, thousands of visitors are attracted to the natural display at Red Rock Canyon. Here, Grinnell argillite has been carved into a deep gorge by water erosion. The adobe red of this rock together with the flow of a clear mountain stream create one of Waterton's striking features.

Historically, this area has long been a congregating spot. Mountain passes at the heads of the two valleys that converge here served as major travel routes for both Indians and, later, explorers. Red Rock Canyon was a traditional campsite for these journeys. Today, Park visitors still gather here to enjoy the area's features and scenery and for access to a number of backcountry trails (see above). There is ample parking for all, and pleasant picnic sites for those who wish to enjoy the interpretive exhibit or the easy strolls around the Canyon itself (29) or to Blakiston Falls (30).

---

29 RED ROCK CANYON LOOP

Trailhead:	Red Rock Canyon
Destination:	Short loop around Red Rock Canyon
Length:	.7 km (.4 mi.) allow 20 minutes
Difficulty Level:	Easy

ACCESS   This loop begins at the Interpretive Exhibit at Red Rock Canyon.

ATTRACTIONS   An easy stroll around Lower Red Rock Canyon, one of Waterton's most impressive geological features. Interpretive display. Bighorn sheep and mule deer are often seen here.

CONSIDERATIONS   This is a high-use area in July and August. Please stay on designated trails to protect the delicate and much abused environment here. Stand back from the edge of the canyon; loose rock makes the rim slippery. Please do not throw rocks.

THE TRAIL   The interpretive exhibit at Red Rock Canyon is a basic course in the geology of this interesting terrain. Like much of the rock in Waterton, the red Grinnell argillite here is from the Precambrian period and among the oldest sedimentary rock on earth. The hard-surfaced path around the lower section of the Canyon is an easy stroll and trailside markers identify features visible here. Bighorn sheep and mule deer often wander through the lodgepole pines that border the trail. Enjoy them, but let them remain wild. Do not try to entice them with food or they may become dependent and be unable to survive the long winter. Foot bridges that cross the Canyon allow fine views into the narrow gorge. Its brick-red argillite rock, exotic pools and miniature waterfalls blend with the green vegetation along the path, making this colorful spot a delight to the eye.

30 BLAKISTON FALLS

Trailhead:	Red Rock Canyon
Destination:	Blakiston Falls overlook
Length:	1 km (.6 mi.) allow ½ hr. one way
Difficulty Level:	Easy

ACCESS From Red Rock Canyon (28), cross the bridge over Lower Red Rock Creek at the Interpretive Display and turn left along the creek.

ATTRACTIONS An easy stroll through cool forest to Blakiston Falls along a wide path with a gentle grade.

CONSIDERATIONS Do not cross the retainer fence at the falls; the rock ledges are very slippery. All facilities are at Red Rock Canyon.

THE TRAIL This wooded trail can offer a pleasant contrast to the activity around Red Rock Canyon. Cross the footbridge over Red Rock Creek and turn hard left onto the trail to Blakiston Falls. After a short distance, a second bridge crosses Bauerman Creek and the path to the right takes you into a lodgepole pine forest. These trees were used by Indians for teepee or lodge poles, giving them their name. The trail through the pines offers a look at a forest in transition. You will notice both here and in other parts of the Park that many of the pine trees are dead. A periodic, natural infestation of the mountain pine bark beetle has killed these trees. As they die and lose their needles, light penetrates the forest floor that had previously been shaded. This additional light stimulates faster growth of fir and spruce as well as the undergrowth of grasses and leafy shrubs, which provides new forage for wildlife. Eventually the dead pines fall to the forest floor and their decomposition adds nutrients to the soil from which they grew. Learn more about Waterton's forests from the pamphlet *The Trees and Forests of Waterton Lakes National Park*, available at the Information Bureau.

The trail reaches its destination at Blakiston Falls. Railed steps and platforms allow you a bird's-eye view of the falls that spill over hard sedimentary rock from deep pools in red and green argillite. Benches invite you to sit awhile and enjoy the sights and sounds around you. Rushing water, the smell of the pines and, maybe, the sight of a forest-dwelling goshawk can all be part of the day. On the way back, you can take an alternate trail 200 metres from the platform. This route rejoins the main trail near the bridge at Bauerman Creek.

31 BLAKISTON VALLEY

Trailhead:	Red Rock Canyon
Destination:	Blakiston Valley junction
Length:	10.1 km (6.3 mi.) allow 2 to 3 hrs. one way
Difficulty Level:	Moderately easy

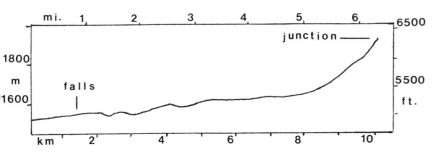

ACCESS The Blakiston Valley Trail is a continuation of the Blakiston Falls Trail (30) which begins at Red Rock Canyon (28) parking lot. This trail is also accessible from the south via Lone Lake Trail (41) and from the north via Blue Grouse Basin Trail (40).

ATTRACTIONS Significant historical route. Terminates at major junction.

CONSIDERATIONS No facilities.

THE TRAIL The wide, open Blakiston Valley, which runs from the South Kootenay Pass through the mountains and out to the prairies, has for centuries provided an easy travel route through the southern Rocky Mountains. Archeologists believe this route was first used by prehistoric nomadic people who travelled through the valley hunting and gathering the rich variety of plants and animals in the area. The Kootenai Indians regularly journeyed through here to hunt buffalo. It was they who revealed this route to Lt. Thomas Blakiston who made the first recorded crossing in 1858. Today, hikers and riders continue to travel this trail for access to the western regions of Waterton Park.

The Blakiston Valley Trail continues along the north bank of Blakiston Creek from the Falls. The travelling is easy as you move through patches of sparse forest and across grassy avalanche tracks. Mount Blakiston and Mount Hawkins tower to the south while Anderson Peak and Lost Mountain rise to the north. The valley forks around Lone Mountain and the trail leaves Blakiston Creek to follow Lone Creek 3.7 km to the Blakiston Valley Junction. A major crossroads, Blakiston Valley Junction is an important point of reference for travel in this area. From here the South Kootenay Pass Trail (32) continues steeply west; the Blue Grouse Basin Trail (40) to Twin Lakes (38) heads north, to the right; and the Lone Lake Trail (41) which connects with the Tamarack Trail (18) is south to the left.

32 SOUTH KOOTENAY PASS

Trailhead:	Blakiston Junction
Destination:	South Kootenay Pass; Park border with B.C.
Length:	1.7 km (1 mi.) allow 1 hr. one way
Difficulty Level:	Moderately easy

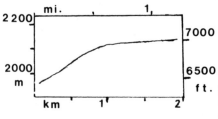

ACCESS The South Kootenay pass is an extension of the Blakiston Valley Trail (31), and branches west off the Lone Lake Trail (41) 100 metres from the Blakiston junction.

ATTRACTIONS Historical mountain pass. Access to routes into British Columbia's Kishinena area.

CONSIDERATIONS No facilities. Return by same route. Routes beyond Park border are not maintained or well-marked.

THE TRAIL This short trail to South Kootenay Pass is a steep climb up a treed slope to the Continental Divide. The trail goes part way up Kishinena Peak and then curves south about 1 km to the pass. This pass and the trail leading from the Rocky Mountain trench out to the prairies along Blakiston Creek (known locally as Pass Creek) have been used for over 8000 years. The Kootenay people of what is now southeastern B.C. called it the Buffalo Trail. Routes from this border of Waterton Lakes National Park continue on into B.C., but logging of beetle-killed pines has been extensive and these routes may be hard to follow. Those who wish to continue further should purchase the National Topographic Survey map *Sage Creek* (B.C.) 82 G/1 or consult B.C. Parks at Nelson or, in the summer months, at the headquarters on the Forum Lake Trail (19).

---

33 SNOWSHOE

Trailhead:	Red Rock Canyon
Destination:	Snowshoe Cabin
Length:	8.2 km (5.1 mi.) allow 2 to 3 hrs. one way
Difficulty Level:	Easy

ACCESS The Snowshoe Trail begins at the Red Rock Canyon parking lot. Cross the footbridge closest to the parking lot and continue straight along the trail to the west up Bauerman Valley.

ATTRACTIONS Major access route for several backcountry destinations. Easy trail along a wide valley floor.

CONSIDERATIONS No facilities before Snowshoe Cabin. The trail is open in places to the full effects of the sun. Carry water.

THE TRAIL Snowshoe Trail is the major access route for several trails in the northwest corner of Waterton Park. Originally a fire and service road to the Snowshoe warden patrol cabin, this route is now accessible only to hikers, riders, and cyclists. The old roadbed makes a good base for this wide easy trail. It leaves Red Rock Canyon and drops into an open meadow alongside Bauerman Creek. Pyramid-shaped Anderson Peak rises 2683 metres on the south side of the stream. At 4.6 km along the route, the Goat Lake Trail (34) branches right. The Snowshoe Trail continues along the valley floor and slopes gently uphill to Snowshoe Cabin. A backcountry campsite area, Snowshoe Cabin is also a major trail junction for Lost Lake (36), Castle River Divide (35), Twin Lakes (38), and the Avion Ridge Route (37).

34 GOAT LAKE

Trailhead: Snowshoe Trail
Destination: Goat Lake
Length: 2.5 km (1.5 mi.) allow 1 to 2 hrs. one way
Difficulty Level: Moderately difficult

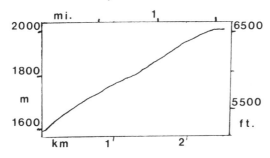

ACCESS From Red Rock Canyon (28), you must travel 3.8 km (2 mi.) along the Snowshoe Trail (33). A sign indicates the junction with the Goat Lake Trail.

ATTRACTIONS Mountain goats on the wall above the lake. The meadow here is superb alpine flower habitat.

CONSIDERATIONS A steep grade from the junction with Snowshoe Trail; much of the trail traverses an open rocky slope. Travel early and avoid mid-day heat. Carry water. Fishing poor. Return by same route. **HORSES:** The trail into Goat Lake is steep and riders may wish to lead their mounts.

THE TRAIL The steep climb into this high mountain lake begins as soon as you leave Snowshoe Trail. Switchbacks across a scree and bedrock slope on an open mountainside create a demanding ascent in the summer sun, but a rejuvenating waterfall rewards your efforts as you reach the lip of the basin. The lake is tucked against a steep ridge running off Newman Peak and the white mountain goats often seen on this rocky wall give the lake its name.

Mountain goats are not technically goats, but are actually of the mountain antelope family. They are extraordinarily well-adapted to a year-round life on the high cliffs of these mountains. Their bodies are narrow and allow for easy mobility along precarious ledges. Their hooves are remarkably well-adapted for sure footing on steep cliffs that appear to have no footholds at all; rough pliant soles offer good grip and the hooves splay out with each step for balance. The mountain goat's hair grows long, thick and hollow-tubed for insulation and covers a wooly under-fur for protection against the severe climate at these elevations. Be sure to bring your binoculars for a close look at these marvellous mountain creatures.

Goat Lake's alpine meadows are a flower lover's delight in July and early August. The bright colors of Indian paintbrush, blue lupines, yellow columbines and purple silky phacelia combine with arnicas, monkey flowers, tiny forget-me-nots and many more to create a carpet of flowers around the basin. Once stocked with rainbow and cutthroat trout, Goat Lake now holds only small, but plentiful, cutthroat. Avion Ridge may be reached from Goat Lake but is not recommended. The access route is very steep, unmarked, and not maintained. See Avion Ridge (37).

35 CASTLE RIVER DIVIDE

Trailhead:	Snowshoe Cabin
Destination:	Northwest border of Waterton
Length:	2.9 km (1.8 mi.) allow 1 hr. one way
Difficulty Level:	Moderately easy

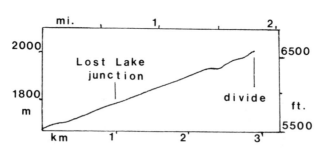

ACCESS From Snowshoe Cabin on the Snowshoe Trail (33), the Castle River Divide Trail branches right and travels northwest up the main valley.

ATTRACTIONS Access to the Avion Ridge Route (37) and the Castle River drainage beyond the Park boundary.

CONSIDERATIONS No facilities. Return by same route.

THE TRAIL From the Snowshoe Cabin, the Castle River Divide Trail continues up a treed valley to a low pass on the northwest boundary of Waterton Park. Historically this pass was used by Indians and explorers, and is still used today for travel into the Castle River drainage, and out to Beaver Mines. However, clear-cut logging has altered this once strikingly beautiful valley and routes into the Castle River are not maintained. Topographical map, NTS *Sage Creek* 82 G/1 is recommended for travel beyond the Park boundary or consult B.C. Parks.

36 LOST LAKE

Trailhead: Castle River Divide Trail
Destination: Lost Lake
Length: .9 km (.6 mi.) allow ½ hr. one way
Difficulty Level: Easy

ACCESS From Snowshoe Cabin on the Snowshoe Trail (33), travel the Castle River Divide Trail (35). Approximately 1 km (.8 mi.) beyond the cabin, the Lost Lake Trail branches left and west.

ATTRACTIONS Beautiful backcountry trail into side valley. Good short hike for Snowshoe Cabin campers.

CONSIDERATIONS No facilities. Return by same route.

THE TRAIL This seldom-used trail travels below a steep ridge extending from the Continental Divide. A short, easy trail, Lost Lake provides a picturesque destination for hikers and riders exploring this region of the Park.

Like many of the slopes in Waterton's mountain basins, the steep, scoured face behind Lost Lake is regularly ravaged by avalanches. Avalanches are a powerful natural phenomenon. Tons of snow accumulates in pockets on the mountainsides and, with the right combination of weight, weather and slope, can break loose and slide at speeds up to 200 km per hour, carrying rocks and trees along with it. Once an avalanche is moving, wind blasts that precede it can blow down trees in its path. In basins such as this one containing Lost Lake, avalanches may smash through ice, sweeping water right out of the lake.

Many high lakes in Waterton have been stocked in the past; but, as in Lost Lake, avalanche kill has eliminated the fish populations. Unless fishing is your prime purpose, Lost Lake is still a pleasant objective and an interesting place to study the effects of avalanches.

37 AVION RIDGE ROUTE

Trailhead:	Castle River Divide
Destination:	Hikers: Goat Lake basin or Yarrow basin. Riders: Se Considerations below.
Length:	To Goat Lake: 8 km (5 mi.) allow 4 to 5 hrs. from the D vide Trail one way
	To Yarrow Basin: 16 km (10 mi.) allow 8 hrs. from the D vide Trail one way
Difficulty Level:	Moderately difficult

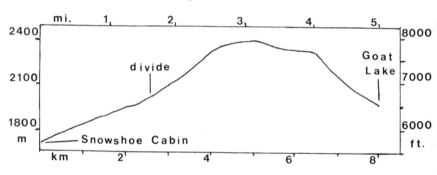

ACCESS From Snowshoe Cabin, travel the Castle River Divide Trail (35). The Avion Ridge Route departs to the right (east) from the top of the pass.

ATTRACTIONS A beautiful skyline ridge run with unlimited views.

CONSIDERATIONS This seldom-travelled route is not maintained and may be hard to follow. Check with the Information Bureau about conditions. Much of the distance along this high ridge offers no protection from bad weather or wind and travellers are especially vulnerable to hypothermia. Carry extra clothing, even on sunny days. Visual navigation is essential and the route becomes difficult to follow in cloudy conditions. Travel across loose scree slopes here can be difficult; experience is recommended. Carry water.
HORSES: Do not attempt to descend into Goat Lake. Proceed out to Yarrow Valley, but be aware that this route demands exact knowledge of the route across steep, loose

scree slopes. Horses should be led across steep sections.

THE ROUTE The Avion Ridge Route junction with the Castle River Divide Trail is not well-defined. At the Park boundary, the route ascends to the east through a series of alpine larch stands and open meadows carpeted with mountain sedges and wildflowers. The route follows the Park boundary and curves along Avion Ridge across red argillite scree slopes.

Travelling on scree slopes requires caution. Patches of scree are unstable and can move underfoot. Look for a defined hikers' route or game trails where the rock is slightly packed and somewhat more stable. Travel single file, walk upright to minimize sliding, and place your feet carefully.

Good visibility is essential for navigating this ridge and you should pick a clear, calm day. You will want to see all you can of the sweeping views from this high vantage point. The trail traverses below the southeast face of Newman Peak. Continue along the mountainside until most of Goat Lake is visible to the south before beginning the descent into the basin. The descent route is steep and undefined and switchbacks down the left (north) side of Goat Lake basin. You must negotiate your way around two bands of rock outcroppings which form small cliffs, rather than attempting to go over them.

As an alternative route from Newman Peak, hikers can travel north and descend to an unnamed lake in Yarrow Basin. From the lake, an abandoned seismic road leads 5.6 km (3.5 mi.) to a gas well site, then another 3.2 km (2 mi.) to a locked gate where pre-arranged vehicle transport can wait. Service vehicles may be encountered beyond the well site.

38 TWIN LAKES

Trailhead: Snowshoe Cabin
Destination: Twin Lakes Basin
Length: 3.2 km (2.0 mi.) from Snowshoe Cabin, allow 1 to 2 hrs. one way
Difficulty Level: Moderately easy

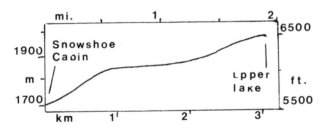

ACCESS From Red Rock Canyon, travel the Snowshoe Trail (33) 8.2 km (5.1 mi.). At the Snowshoe Cabin Junction, the Twin Lakes Trail crosses the stream on a footbridge and climbs to the southwest. Twin Lakes may also be reached via the Blakiston Valley (31) and Blue Grouse (40) Trails. It may also be included on the Tamarack Tour (18).

ATTRACTIONS Moderately easy trail to a remote area. Beautiful alpine setting with camping facilities and fishing for brook trout.

CONSIDERATIONS Twin Lakes campsite provides a useful facility that enhances your backcountry experience. Help keep it clean by packing out all that you pack in. **HORSES:** Please tie horses away from kitchen and camp area.

THE TRAIL Twin Lakes is at the head of a valley 3 km from the junction at Snowshoe Cabin; the trail leaves there via a footbridge over the outflow creek from Lost Lake. It gains altitude in a series of short switchbacks through mature spruce forest before it levels out into a picturesque open valley often subject to winter avalanches. The slopes of Mount Bauerman to the south are ribboned with avalanche tracks that meet the trail in grassy meadows. At the end of the valley bottom, the trail steepens again as it re-enters the forest and climbs to Upper Twin Lake. Camping facilities are located in a grassy meadow adjacent to Upper Twin Lake. Lower Twin is reached by a trail beyond the campsite.

Stands of beargrass line the trail to Twin Lakes. Waterton is near the northern limit for this species, *Xerophyllum tenax*. A large, striking plant, its cone of small white

71

flowers or, later, a spike of seeds, tops a long straight stem. At the base is a clump of sharp-edged leaves that look like grass, but the plant is really a member of the lily family. Elk and small rodents feed on the upper plant and the tough grassy leaves are used by grizzly bears to line their dens.

The trip to Twin Lakes offers a traveller a variety of terrain from forest to meadow to alpine lakes set against the sheer cliffs of the Continental Divide.

39 SAGE PASS

Trailhead: Twin Lakes Trail
Destination: Sage Pass and the western border of Waterton Park
Length: 1.4 km (.9 mi.) allow 1 hr. one way
Difficulty Level: Moderately difficult

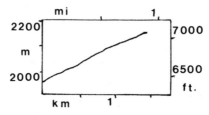

ACCESS Travel the Snowshoe Trail (33) 8.2 km from Red Rock Canyon to the Snowshoe Cabin. Another 2.9 km along the Twin Lakes Trail (38), the Sage Pass Trail branches to the right.

ATTRACTIONS Short trail onto the Continental Divide. Access to ridge tops that form the Divide.

CONSIDERATIONS Sage Pass marks the Park boundary and the B.C. border. Routes beyond Sage Pass are not marked and are not well-defined. For travel on ridge routes, purchase NTS topographical map "Sage Creek" 82 G/1 for the area.

THE TRAIL It is a short steep climb through open subalpine forest and around rock ledges to Sage Pass where a cairn at the summit marks the Continental Divide.

Known as the geological backbone of North America, the divide runs for over three thousand miles from South America to Alaska, separating the waters of western Canada between the Pacific and Arctic watersheds. Waters draining to the east cross the prairies through the Saskatchewan River system and flow into Hudson Bay through the Nelson River. Waters on the British Columbia side enter the Pacific Ocean through the Columbia River drainage.

Unmarked routes from Sage Pass take you along the Divide. To the north, a route travels to Faunt Mountain and beyond along the B.C.-Alberta border. To the south, another route offers unobstructed vertical views into Twin Lakes Basin. Both routes are exposed, high-mountain terrain and require pathfinding skills.

40 BLUE GROUSE BASIN
(Pecks Basin)

Trailhead: Twin Lakes
Destination: Blakiston Valley Junction
Length: 3.3 km (2 mi.) allow 1 to 1-1/2 hrs. one way
Difficulty Level: Moderately easy

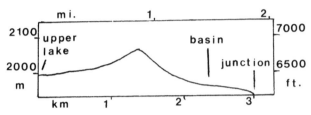

ACCESS From Red Rock Canyon, Blue Grouse Basin may be reached via the Snowshoe (33) and Twin Lakes (38) trails, or the Blakiston Valley Trail (31). If approaching from the south along the Lone Lake Trail (41), pick up Blue Grouse at the Blakiston Valley Junction.

ATTRACTIONS Fine view above Twin Lakes.

CONSIDERATIONS No facilities. **HORSES:** Snow may persist here until late summer. Check with the Information Bureau.

THE TRAIL The Blue Grouse Basin Trail is a link between Twin Lakes and the Blakiston Valley Trail. As you leave the Twin Lakes Basin and traverse the scree slope below the Continental Divide, the view extends the length of Bauerman Creek Valley to Red Rock Canyon with Cloudy Ridge and Mount Glendowan in the background. The trail passes through a beautiful stand of alpine larch as it tops a rock ledge that has been blasted out to allow safer passage. It then drops into a small basin centered around a shallow lake and travels through meadow and forest to the junction with Blakiston Valley (31) and Lone Lake (41) trails.

The north and east slopes of this basin, like many others in the Park, are excellent grizzly bear denning habitat. In fall, most Waterton grizzlies dig their dens on high mountain slopes at elevations between 1800 and 2300 metres. They choose slopes sheltered from the sun and wind to insure a heavy snow cover that will last through the winter, insulating them from extreme cold and protecting them from warm Chinook winds that could melt a thinner snow blanket.

41 LONE LAKE

Trailhead: Blakiston Junction
Destination: Lone Lake
Length: 4.2 km (2.6 mi.) from Blakiston Junction, allow 1 to 1-1/2 hrs. for this section one way
Difficulty Level: Easy

ACCESS The Lone Lake Trail branches south from the junction at the end of the Blakiston Valley Trail (31). It may also be approached from the south via Tamarack Trail (18), and from the north via the Blue Grouse Trail (40).

ATTRACTIONS Trail parallels the Continental Divide. Cutthroat fishing.

CONSIDERATIONS Return by same route. Lone Lake is often travelled as part of the longer Tamarack Tour. This requires adequate preparation and previous planning. See Tamarack Trail (18).

THE TRAIL The trail into Lone Lake is well-defined and graded for easy travel. As you hike south from the Blakiston Valley Junction, your route parallels the Continental Divide. To the west, steep scree slopes rise to meet this long unbroken escarpment. Occasional large spruce which have withstood the force of avalanches stand tall along the slope.

Lone Lake is perched on a narrow bench in a small basin of bedrock and its outlet creek plunges immediately over a cliff.

Layers of tilted sedimentary rock extend into the lake, creating a convoluted western shoreline. Cutthroat trout do well in these cold waters. Backcountry camping facilities are on the southwest side of the lake near the trail.

One of Waterton's features is its abundant wildlife. The scree slopes and meadows around Lone Lake are part of the summer range of bighorn rams. Unlike mountain goats, bighorn sheep spend the winter congregated at lower elevations, but, come summer, most rams leave the ewes and lambs and head for the high alpine regions. The rams' thick, curving horns are the distinguishing feature of the bighorn and the rings on these horns can be read like a diary. The corrugations around the horn reflect the conditions during each yearly cycle. An annual ring, often indented or darker, represents the two or more months during the winter when food is so scarce that the animals live on body fat. Between these rings are one-half to six inches of growth reflecting the good months, with most growth in mid-summer. The shorter spaces between annual rings show the effects of drought, sickness or old age.

From winter mountaineering to easy set tracks, Waterton offers a variety of Nordic skiing.

On the Prince of Wales Trail.

Along the Akamina Parkway.

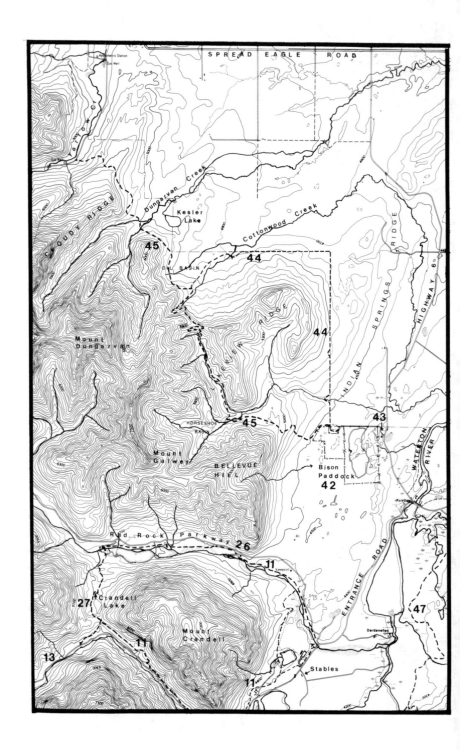

BISON PADDOCKS

78

42 BISON PADDOCKS

TRAILHEAD FOR:
Bison Viewpoint (43), Horseshoe Basin (45), and Park Line (44).

The Bison Paddock is located 10 km from Waterton townsite, or 2 km north of the main Park entrance kiosk along Alberta Highway 6. A small herd of enclosed plains bison grazes in a paddock on the Park boundary at this access point. Outside the Park, grasslands that once maintained thousands of bison are now pasture for beef cattle herds. Southern Alberta is a major producer of beef, and cowboys still work the herds on the rolling hillsides surrounding the Park. Only a fence separates the old and the new, public park and private ranchland. Waterton is one of a very few Canadian designated Biosphere Reserves, part of an international network in a UNESCO-sponsored program which seeks to integrate conservation of natural resources with their use by man. Here the boundary fence marks the demarcation between the protected core area (park) and the zone of cooperation (ranchlands). Together mutual needs and problems can be studied and a balance struck where differences once existed. A combined effort of landowners and Park personnel, the Waterton Biosphere Reserve strives to maintain the natural beauty and sustained use of this area. For more information, contact the Park superintendent.

43 BISON VIEWPOINT

Trailhead:	Bison Paddocks
Destination:	Bison Viewpoint Exhibit
Length:	300 metres (330 yds.) allow 10 minutes one way
Difficulty Level:	Easy

ACCESS Trail begins at the Bison Paddock parking lot located just off Highway 6 north, 2 km from the Park entrance kiosk.

ATTRACTIONS Easy stroll to a dramatic viewpoint overlooking mountains and prairies, including bison summer range and elk winter range. Viewing scope at the end of the trail.

CONSIDERATIONS Can be unpleasant on windy days. Return by same route.

THE TRAIL This easy stroll along a wide, paved path takes you to the edge of one of Waterton's unique areas. An expanse of shortgrass prairie, this was once part of the home range for large herds of bison. When Kootenai Brown first arrived in the area in 1865, he wrote: ''Emerging from the South Kootenay Pass, we hit the foothills near the mouth of Pass Creek [Blakiston] and climbed to the top of one of the lower mountains. The prairie as far as we could see east, north and west was one living mass of buffalo.'' Before the end of the nineteenth century the bison were nearly exterminated by hunters. In 1952, a small number of plains bison were reintroduced to this rolling prairie, their natural habitat.

During late spring and summer, the bison graze on the fescue prairie in a drive-through paddock that allows visitors to see these majestic animals in their natural surroundings. People must stay in their cars and the road is not open to pedestrians or cyclists. In winter, the herd is moved to a smaller enclosure just to the west where trees provide shelter from the severe blizzards that blow across these open prairies.

44 PARK LINE TRAIL

Trailhead: Bison Paddocks
Destination: Oil Basin
Length: 9.6 km (6 mi.) allow 2 to 3 hrs. one way
Difficulty Level: Moderately easy
Notice: This is no longer maintained as a Park Trail.

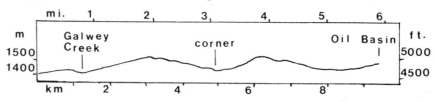

ACCESS A road extends along the north side of the bison enclosure to a narrow gate which allows access to hikers and riders.

ATTRACTIONS Travels the northeast boundary of the Park. View of private prairie ranchland to the east. Connects with Horseshoe Trail (45) in Oil Basin for a good loop route.

CONSIDERATIONS Considerable hunting takes place on private lands adjacent to the trail in the spring and fall; wear bright-colored clothing. Carry water. Return by same route or connect with Horseshoe Basin Trail (45) for loop back to trailhead. **HORSES:** Trailers may have difficulty turning on access road; park in Bison Viewpoint parking lot.

THE TRAIL At the gate, a short trail circles a small slough and meets the Park Line Trail. It then leads north (to the right) paralleling the Park Boundary fence along the east flank of Lakeview Ridge and allows easy access for off-trail exploration of the hillside. As the trail rises above the prairie, small lakes and sloughs become visible. These provide excellent waterfowl habitat and are characteristic of this landscape. At a point 4.8 km (3 mi.) from the access gate the trail makes a 90° turn and heads straight west toward jagged Mount Dungarvan. Moose and elk can often be seen in the swampy terrain below the trail and bears sometimes cross the road here, travelling from coniferous forest above the road to poplar bottom below. The trail soon drops down to the flat grass-lands of Oil Basin where it connects with the Horseshoe Trail at the wardens' patrol cabin. Oil Basin, with its grassy hillsides and poplar bluffs, is the fall and winter habitat of one of the two elk herds in the Park. The males, weighing as much as 700 kg, can be heard bugling their mating calls during the rutting season in September. This silvery sound can make a chilly fall hike seem well worth the effort.

45 HORSESHOE BASIN

Trailhead: Bison Paddocks
Destination: Oil Basin or Yarrow Creek
Length: To Oil Basin 10.6 km (6.6 mi.) allow 3 to 4 hrs. one way
To Yarrow Creek 15.7 km (9.8 mi.) allow 5 to 7 hrs. one way
Difficulty Level: Moderately difficult

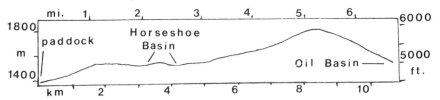

ACCESS From the Bison Paddocks (42) continue down the service road. A narrow gate at the end of the road allows access for hikers and riders.

ATTRACTIONS Travels both prairie and mountain terrain. Elk winter range. Good horse trail.

CONSIDERATIONS Very dry area, carry water. Return by same trail or connect with Park Line Trail (44) for return to trailhead. Yarrow Creek route beyond Oil Basin is poorly marked and difficult to follow; hikers and riders using this route may wish to arrange pick-up at Yarrow Creek Road via Spread Eagle Road. **HORSES:** Trailers may have difficulty turning around on access road. Park at Bison Viewpoint parking lot.

THE TRAIL From the access gate beyond the Bison Paddocks, follow the trail around a small slough. The Horseshoe Trail branches left and heads west as it curves around the Bison Paddock corrals. Several reliable springs meet the trail along this section. Known as Indian Springs, this area was commonly used as a campsite by native people. The trail is not well-defined beyond the corrals and a watchful eye is re-

quired to follow the path across a grassy hillside to a trail sign. As poplar forest closes in, the trail once again becomes obvious as it climbs to the crest of a shoulder of Bellevue Hill and offers sweeping views across the prairie to the mountains of Waterton and Glacier. The trail heads across a grassy meadow and the steep east side of Mount Galwey rises ahead. After crossing Galwey Brook, which is often dry in summer, the trail turns north along a treeless valley bottom. This mountain valley on the edge of prairie grasslands provides excellent habitat for a number of wildlife species including elk, mule deer, bighorn sheep, cougar and bear.

A series of switchbacks assists travellers to reach a saddle between Mount Galwey and Lakeview Ridge before the trail descends along a small ravine onto an open hillside in Oil Basin. Here, it splits at a poorly-defined junction. To the right, the path proceeds to the warden patrol cabin and connects with the Park Line Trail (44) for return to the Bison Paddocks (9.6 km). To the left, it winds west to the Park boundary at Yarrow Creek (4.5 km). This second route is difficult to follow – it passes above and west of Kesler Lake and continues around the base of a rocky ridge before it drops down into poplar forest to cross the two forks of Dungarvan Creek above their junction. After a long climb across a grassy slope, the trail crests on a shoulder of Cloudy Ridge. A blaze mark on a large pine directs you left into heavy forest and the trail switchbacks down to the Park boundary and Yarrow Creek Road.

Horse travel on remote routes requires good preparation.

46 CHIEF MOUNTAIN HIGHWAY

TRAILHEAD FOR:
Vimy Peak (47), Bosporus (48) and Belly River (49) trails; access to Belly River Campgrounds; Glacier National Park (50) and U.S. Customs. Overland route to Crypt Lake (12).

Chief Mountain International Highway provides access to the eastern regions of Waterton Lakes National Park and is the main summer roadway between it and Glacier National Park in the United States. The highway branches southeast from Alberta Highway 5 one kilometre east of the main Park entrance kiosk. It rises quickly above the prairie lowlands to a fine viewpoint 7 km along the roadway. Interpretive plaques here and the pamphlet *Mountains and Valleys* (available at the Information Centre) explain the geology of the features visible from this vantage point.

Sofa Mountain dominates the skyline to the south as the roadway continues. Classified as wildlands, this area remains little changed by man and natural processes continue here as they have for thousands of years. At 8 km, a pullout entices you to stop alongside one of the many ponds and sloughs visible from the highway. An inhabited beaver lodge provides travellers with an opportunity to view these industrious creatures who are instrumental in the creation of this type of landscape.

The Lookout Butte picnic site at 9.5 km offers a pleasant resting area with cold spring water and washrooms. A kilometre farther, the highway enters part of the Blood Indian Timber Reserve. The main reserve lies further to the east on open prairie. Set aside in the original treaty with the British, this heavily-wooded tract of lodgepole pines supplied the tribe with teepee poles. To the south, Chief Mountain rises above the valley. Standing in solitude, it has long held spiritual significance for the entire Blackfeet nation, of which the Bloods are a tribe. As the highway re-enters Waterton Park, it drops down and crosses the Belly River. Two kilometres ahead, the access road for Belly River Campground is on the right.

Sweeping views into Glacier's Belly River drainage are possible at a pullout a short distance farther along the highway. A Glacier Park topographical map (available at the Waterton Park Information Centre) together with binoculars can provide interesting visual exploration from this viewpoint.

In less than two kilometres, the Chief Mountain Highway meets the 49th parallel, the International Boundary. Here Chief Mountain Customs is open during limited hours in the summer season from mid-May to mid-September. You should check with the Information Centre or Customs |(403) 382-2603| to confirm dates and times. The customs crossing at Carway, south of Cardston, is open year round.

47 VIMY PEAK

Trailhead: Chief Mountain International Highway
Destination: Eastern slope of Vimy Peak
Length: 13.9 km (8.7 mi.) allow 5 to 6 hrs. one way
Difficulty Level: To Stoney Creek Flats (first half) - Easy. To mountainside (second half) - Moderately difficult.

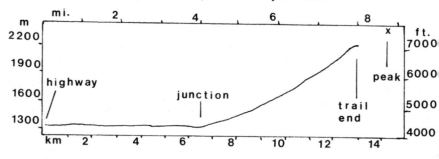

ACCESS Vimy Peak Trail departs south from Chief Mountain Highway (46) .5 km from its junction with Alberta Highway 5. Vimy Peak Trail may also be reached via the Bosporus Trail (48); boaters may wish to cross Middle Waterton Lake to the Wishbone boat landing for access to Vimy Peak. **HORSES:** The Vimy Peak Trail may also be reached by crossing the Waterton River at the Dardanelles, connecting with the trail on Stoney Creek Flats. This crossing should only be attempted after all danger of high water has passed. Check with the Information Centre.

ATTRACTIONS First 2.8 km an easy stroll through mixed deciduous forest, providing an excellent spring and fall trail. This section is also good on cloudy or windy days. Superb wildlife habitat. Elk winter range. Migratory waterfowl viewing. Access to top of Vimy Peak (except for cyclists).

CONSIDERATIONS This trail is seldom travelled and sections beyond the first 2.8 km are not well defined and may be difficult to follow. The trail ends below the peak of the mountain. Return by same route. Routes to the summit are not main-

tained trails. Peak is exposed to wind and sudden weather changes. Be prepared; carry water. Check with Park Information Centre if travelling the second section. **CYCLISTS:** Cycling is allowed on the first part of the trail only. Trail may be closed seasonally due to wildlife concerns. Check at the Information Centre for details.

THE TRAIL The Vimy Peak Trail follows an old wagon road through dense aspen and poplar forest. From its beginning, game signs are everywhere. Soft ground may reveal the tracks of moose, elk, deer, wolverine, coyote, bear or lynx. Deciduous trees along the trail also tell the story of animals passing. Moose and elk strip bark to eat in winter, and claw marks record where black bears have climbed. These black scars grow larger as the aspen matures, and last for the life of the tree.

Briefly, the trail breaks out into the open near the shore of Lower Waterton Lake, a good point for observing the many species of waterfowl that congregate here during spring and fall migrations. A little further through the aspens, the trail reaches Stoney Creek Flats, a magnificent expanse of open grass, which provides an unobstructed view of Vimy Peak rising directly ahead. The trail fades into the grass in places, but a trail marker stands above the flat plain as a point of reference. Soon after crossing Sofa Creek and re-entering the forest the trail branches. At 6.2 km it joins with the Bosporus Trail (48) to Wishbone Campsite and Crypt Landing. The Vimy Peak Trail branches east (left) and begins the long steep climb up the mountainside. The forest quickly changes from deciduous to mixed to coniferous as the trail climbs the eastern shoulder of Vimy Peak, passing beneath an impressive limestone outcropping known as the Lion's Head. Switchbacks along a subalpine creek bring you to the trail end in a small basin at 2100 metres. Undefined routes continue from here to the summit at 2347 metres. The view from the Peak encompasses jagged mountain peaks to the west; a bird's eye view into Crypt Basin; and beyond to the highest peak in the Peace Park, 3190-metre Mount Cleveland. To the east overlooking the prairies with binoculars, you may pick out buildings in Lethbridge, 120 km away.

48 BOSPORUS

Trailhead:	Vimy Peak Trail
Destination:	Crypt Landing
Length:	7 km (4.3 mi.) from Vimy Junction, allow 2 to 3 hrs. one way
Difficulty Level:	Easy

ACCESS From the Chief Mountain Highway, hike the Vimy Peak Trail (47). At 6.2 km, the Bosporus Trail branches right (south). Hikers with boat transportation may reach the Bosporus Trail at Crypt Landing (12) on Upper Waterton Lake or at Wishbone boat dock on the southeast side of Middle Waterton Lake. **HORSES:** See Vimy Peak Trail access.

ATTRACTIONS Hike beneath Vimy's north face. Travel across interesting limestone ridge. Trilliums in May. Access for lakeshore fishing from Victoria Day to Labor Day.

CONSIDERATIONS Seldom travelled. Can be very windy. Carry water. Return by same route or arrange boat transportation.

THE TRAIL After leaving Vimy Peak Trail, the Bosporus Trail winds along Middle Waterton Lake through beautiful aspen forest and across rock debris from the face of Waterton's distinctive Vimy Peak. White trilliums grow here, the only place in Alberta this lovely flower is found.

Wishbone campsite at 3.8 km offers camping with dock facilities for boaters. From Wishbone, the trail switchbacks onto a limestone ridge. Once part of a solid rock wall that reached across to Bear's Hump on Mount Crandell, this ridge is all that is left after the wall was ground down by the force of the massive Waterton glacier. The undulating surface of this wind-scoured ridge creates a unique landscape of grassy ledges and shallow valleys.

Tiny Loon Lake occupies a small meadow below the ridge to the west. A short spur trail extends 1.2 km northwest to the Bosporus, a narrow channel connecting Upper and Middle Waterton Lakes. There is good lakeshore fishing here, especially for lake trout.

The main trail continues 2.2 km to Crypt Landing through a forest of limber pine, subalpine fir and Douglas fir. The bent and twisted shapes of these trees is the result of the high winds that frequently funnel down Waterton Lake.

49 BELLY RIVER

Trailhead:	Belly River Campground
Destination:	Park Boundary – Canada-U.S. Border
Length:	2.9 km (1.8 mi.) allow 1 hr. one way
Difficulty Level:	Easy

ACCESS   The trail leaves from the large clearing at the southeast end of the Belly River Campground.

ATTRACTIONS   Easy hike for campers here. Access to Belly River: fishing. Abundant birdlife. View bugling elk in fall.

CONSIDERATIONS   The trail ends at the International Boundary. Return by the same route. Hikers and riders wishing to enter the U.S. must do so from the Chief Mountain Customs Station. See Chief Mountain Highway (46). No facilities on trail.

THE TRAIL   The Belly River Trail departs from the Belly River Campground and follows an old wagon road to the International Boundary. The path rises above the river through a mixed forest of lodgepole pine and poplar before it drops down to the river bank. As it travels through alternating open meadows and shady groves, pools in the river reflect the high mountains at the head of the valley in Glacier National Park. Northern Glacier's high country is the summer home for a large number of elk known as the International herd. During the fall, this herd migrates down the Belly River to their wintering grounds in Canada. The high, shrill bugle of the male elk in September can only be equalled by the sight of this animal with its impressive antlers.

The trail ends 2.9 km (1.8 mi.) from the campground at the boundary with the United States. A cutline runs east and west along the 49th parallel here and marks the border. Return the way you came.

Lowland aspen record a history of elk and bear activity.

Belly River Valley

50 NORTHERN GLACIER

Northern Glacier is a remote region of Glacier National Park. No roads penetrate its deep, forested valleys and only hiking and horse-back riding trails cross its high mountain slopes. This land remains wilderness; home to bighorn sheep, moose and elk. The grizzly finds refuge here and mountain goats observe human visitors from their lofty ranges. Lowland forests are alive with a rich community of plants and animals and powerful earth-altering glaciers still ebb and flow.

Remote backcountry ranger stations and primitive campsites provide the few conveniences in Northern Glacier. Travellers who journey here come to immerse themselves in the true wilderness community.

Glacier is the U.S. component of the International Peace Park and some regulations differ from those in its Canadian counterpart described in the introductory section.

 ## INFORMATION

Glacier's visitor centre at St. Mary, Montana, is the regional information station for several areas, including Northern Glacier. Open daily from mid-May through September, the St. Mary centre offers free maps and brochures and sells a variety of Park-related publications. Information is available here on trail conditions as are necessary Park permits. This centre can be reached by phone at (406) 732-4424. For year-round information contact Glacier Park Headquarters at (406) 888-5441, or write: The Superintendent, Glacier National Park, West Glacier, MT 59936. Northern Glacier's backcountry ranger stations at Goat Haunt and Belly River have area information as well as backcountry users permits, area maps and current trail reports during summer months.

 ## FIRST AID

This area of Glacier is a remote one and facilities are limited. If in need of emergency assistance, contact any Park personnel; many are first-aiders or have radios and all are trained to handle emergency situations. Both Belly River and Goat Haunt ranger stations are equipped for limited first aid needs and both have radio connections for further assistance.

BACKCOUNTRY USERS PERMIT

All backcountry users intending to **HAVE A FIRE OR CAMP OVERNIGHT** must obtain a backcountry users permit free of charge. These are available at all visitor information centres and backcountry ranger stations.

 ## BACKCOUNTRY CAMPING

There are a number of backcountry camping facilities in Glacier's northern regions. Facilities and regulations vary at each as do the number of campers each site can accommodate. A backcountry users permit must be obtained in person from any ranger station or visitor centre and may be arranged the day before your departure. A copy of the backcountry users guide and camping regulations will give you the necessary information to enjoy the backcountry facilities.

 ## FISHING

Many consider Glacier's fishing to be exceptional and in an effort to maintain wild stock in natural environments, certain regulations have been instituted. Those wishing to fish in the Park must obtain a copy of the regulations from any ranger station or visitor centre. Help to preserve stock by familiarizing yourself with the regulations and guidelines. Be sure to properly dispose of fish entrails.

 ## HORSES

Horses and pack animals cannot pass freely from Waterton to Glacier or vice versa. Animals must be properly certified as having had an E.I.A. (Coggins) test and health inspection from a veterinarian. Border crossings must be made at selected customs stations. For more information contact your nearest customs office.

 ## HORSE CAMPING

Not all Northern Glacier campsites accommodate horses. Consult backcountry camping regulations for those that do before departing. No grazing is allowed in Glacier Park. Riders must carry all horsefeed. And please pack out all that you pack in.

MAPS

Maps are available for Northern Glacier regions on two scales. A large topographical map (1:100,000 scale) covers the entire Park. Smaller quadrangle maps (1:24,000) offer more detail. The larger map allows for easy trip planning, while quadrangle maps are more useful on the trail. Both types are available at ranger stations and visitor centres.

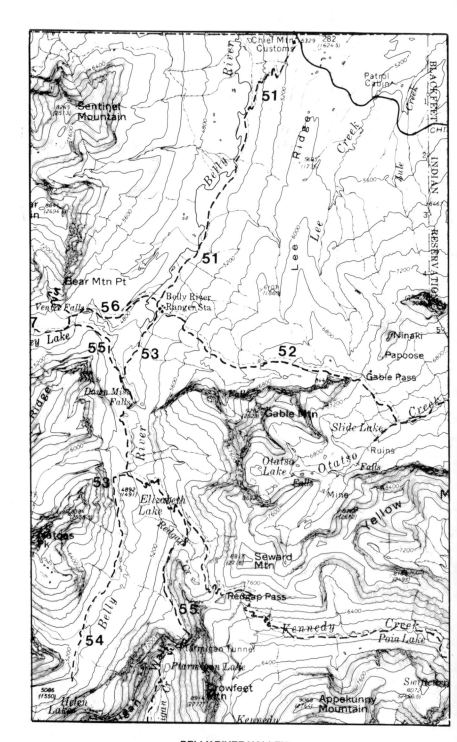

BELLY RIVER VALLEY

90

51 BELLY RIVER VALLEY

Trailhead: Chief Mountain (U.S.) Customs
Destination: Belly River Ranger Station
Length: 10 km (6.2 mi.) allow 2 - 3 hr. one way
Difficulty Level: Moderately easy

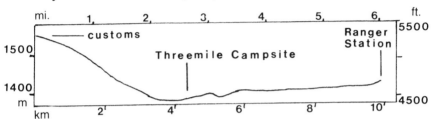

ACCESS The trail begins in the parking lot at the U.S. Customs buildings on the Chief Mountain International Highway (46).

ATTRACTIONS Wildlife and wildflowers on wide valley grasslands. River fishing for trout and whitefish from late May to Nov. 30. Excellent fall hike; bugling elk.

CONSIDERATIONS Glacier Park quadrangle map for Mount Gable is recommended. Open, grassy meadows can be hot at mid-day; travel early. On the return from Belly River ranger station the trail climbs steeply for the final 3.2 km from the valley bottom back up to the customs station. Chief Mountain International Highway Customs Station closes in mid-September. Travellers approaching from Canada must use the Carway port of entry for U.S. access after that time. **HORSES:** Not all U.S. ports of entry can handle horses. For horse access in the U.S. contact your nearest customs office.

THE TRAIL The trail switchbacks down a steep grade from the customs parking lot to the Belly River bottom. The lodgepole pine forest that lined the trail has been thinned by an infestation of mountain pinebark beetle and a healthy understory of subalpine fir and poplar now reaches for the sun that pours through the remaining pines. The trail reaches the Belly River valley and travels to the Threemile backcountry campsite that marks the halfway point to the Belly River ranger station. This riverside campsite area has hitchrails to accommodate riders.

Belly River's lush open meadows of tall timothy and thick bunchgrass extend to the upper reaches of the valley. The trail is relatively level and journeys near the river at times for access to fishing. During the fall large herds of elk gather here for the rut and jousting bulls are a common sight on the grasslands.

As the valley reaches the mountains, the trail arrives at the Belly River ranger station. Here a wooden rail fence that contains the station's pack animals surrounds the rustic station buildings set against Gable Mountain to the southeast. Manned from early May until late September, the ranger station is a major trail junction for this region of the Park. Camping permits are available here as are regulations, information and fishing permits. A campsite near the station accommodates hikers.

The valley forks here around the high walls of Cosley Ridge. To the south, Elizabeth Lake (53) waits to be explored; while the headwall of Mount Cathedral suggests the rugged possibilities of the Stoney Indian Trail (57).

52 GABLE PASS

Trailhead: Belly River Ranger Station
Destination: Slide Lake
Length: 9.8 km (6.1 mi.) allow 4 to 5 hrs. one way
Difficulty Level: Moderately difficult

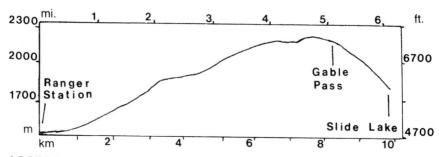

ACCESS The trail begins at the Belly River ranger station on the Belly River Valley Trail (51).

ATTRACTIONS Fine view trail. Cutthroat trout fishing at Slide Lake from late May to Nov. 30. Profuse alpine flowers including the Jones columbine.

CONSIDERATIONS Seldom-travelled trail across alpine ridge. Frequent winds. Trail may be hard to follow above treeline; large stone cairns mark the route. Gable Mountain and Chief Mountain quadrangle maps recommended. Deep snow may remain until late summer; check with Park ranger for conditions.

THE TRAIL The climb from the Belly River ranger station 6.1 km to the summit of Lee Ridge is steep, but this seldom-used trail offers access to fine views of the Belly River and Otatso drainage systems.

The lower section of the trail from the ranger station is typically forested and the steepness of the trail makes for a somewhat tedious climb; but, as you move into the subalpine, wildflowers galore and wide views make the effort worthwhile. The trail winds across the multicolored rocky slope of Gable Mountain which rises directly to the south. To the east, the slab of Chief Mountain shows its southwestern face. Rock cairns direct hikers across this open windswept area. A maze of large boulders lines the trail as it meanders toward the pass. At the summit, Lee Ridge Trail branches left (north) to reach Chief Mountain Highway in 9.6 km. This side trail is seldom-used and little maintained.

The main trail continues another 3.7 km as it quickly descends through dense woods to the foot of Upper Slide Lake. Good fishing is an attraction in these lakes created by a massive rockslide from Yellow Mountain. An unmarked fishermen's path branches right along the shore and ends at the head of the upper lake. Further up the valley in the remote headwaters of the Otatso, several ruins of cabins and a deserted mine are all that remain of the Van Pelt operations that were attempted at the turn of the century.

The main trail branches left to Lower Slide Lake and a small campsite for both hikers and riders. The trail continues another 1.6 km to the Park boundary and border of the Blackfeet Indian Reservation. An old roadbed continues from the boundary to a poor dirt road which reaches the Chief Mountain Highway in 8 km.

53 ELIZABETH LAKE

Trailhead:	Belly River Ranger Station
Destination:	North shore of Elizabeth Lake
Length:	5.5 km (3.4 mi.) allow 1½ to 2 hrs. one way
Difficulty Level:	Moderately easy

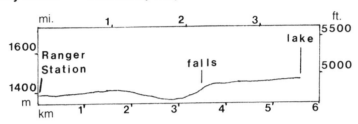

ACCESS From the Belly River ranger station, hikers cross the horse corral meadow to the Elizabeth Lake Trail. **HORSES:** Riders follow the corral fence south and through a wire gate at its far end. Just beyond, a side trail drops down to the Belly River campground. The Elizabeth Lake Trail continues along the top of a grassy bench before entering the trees. Elizabeth Lake may also be approached via the Ptarmigan Trail (55) from Many Glacier to the east and Cosley Lake (56) to the west.

ATTRACTIONS Dawn Mist Falls. Large mountain lake set in deeply-carved glacial valley. Good fishing for rainbow trout and arctic grayling from late May to late November.

CONSIDERATIONS This is excellent bear habitat; fishermen should properly dispose of fish entrails. Gable Mountain quadrangle map recommended. No open fires at Elizabeth campsite. **HORSES:** At 2.5 km along the trail, a horse ford trail branches from the hiking trail to cross the Belly River. The ford is marked with metal stakes and riders should keep them to their right as they make the ford. (Left on the return trip.) Ford may be difficult in early season during high water. Dawn Mist Falls

spur trail is not recommended for horses.

THE TRAIL From the ranger station, the Elizabeth Lake Trail passes briefly through white-barked aspens that are golden in fall before entering the cool green of a dense coniferous forest. At 2.5 km the trail meets the upper reaches of the Belly River and branches. Horseback riders continue straight ahead to the horse ford while hikers branch right to cross the river on a suspension bridge. The Ptarmigan Trail (55) from Cosley Lake joins the trail on the far side and together they continue south. Dawn Mist Falls, a remarkable sight, is another .5 km along the trail. Here, a short spur for hikers extends to a viewpoint beneath these impressive falls that carry the largest volume of water of any falls in Glacier.

The main trail climbs up alongside the falls and an opening in the trees presents another good view. Beyond 2.5 km the trail breaks out of the forest onto the northern shore of Elizabeth Lake. Backcountry campsites here have hitchrails for horse campers. Steep walls contain the lake on both sides. To the east, the Ptarmigan Trail is etched into red cliffs as it climbs high above the valley. The mountainsides to the west often host grazing mountain goats.

---

54 HELEN LAKE

Trailhead: North end of Elizabeth Lake
Destination: Helen Lake
Length: 6.7 km (4.2 mi.) allow 1½ hrs. one way
Difficulty Level: Easy

ACCESS The Helen Lake Trail is a continuation of the Elizabeth Lake Trail (53) and travels south along the western shoreline of Elizabeth Lake.

ATTRACTIONS Alpine lake set against impressive glacier headwall. Mountain goats often visible on cliffs above trail. Good fishing in upper Elizabeth Lake.

CONSIDERATIONS No fish in Helen Lake. Snow may persist until mid-July. Campsite exposed to wind. Gable Mountain and Many Glacier quadrangle maps are recommended. **HORSES:** No horse camping at Helen Lake. Return by same route.

THE TRAIL You can see only part of Elizabeth Lake from its northern shore and a spectacular view of the rest of this lake rewards those who continue on to Helen Lake. As the trail rounds a dog-leg, high steep walls trimmed with ice fields frame the deep blue of upper Elizabeth Lake. The grassy avalanche tracks that meet the trail may be dotted with white mountain goats. The campsite at the head of the lake, 2.4 km along the trail, has grates for open fires, accommodates both hikers and riders, and allows access to good fishing.

The remaining 4.3 km to Helen Lake is a mountain traveller's delight. This easy trail journeys farther up the alpine valley as high mountains close in on three sides. Alpine meadows and patches of fir and spruce provide a green contrast to the steel grey and rich red of the surrounding cliffs. Helen Lake basin is framed by Ptarmigan Wall to the left, Mount Merrit and the Old Sun Glacier to the right, with Ahern Peak and Glacier forming its headwall.

In an effort to protect this delicate mountain environment, hikers only are allowed use of the backcountry campsites at the foot of the lake and no open fires are permitted. A grassy carpet dotted with low-growing fir invites you to sit and glass the open alpine slopes for goats and grizzly who find this mountain basin excellent habitat.

55 PTARMIGAN TRAIL

Trailhead: Cosley Lake
Destination: Many Glacier, northeastern region of Glacier
Length: 21.7 km (13.5 mi.) allow 6 to 8 hrs. one way
Difficulty Level: Moderately difficult

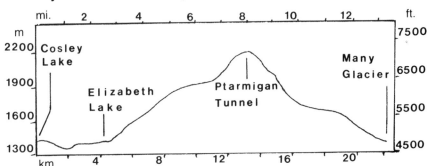

ACCESS The Ptarmigan Trail is a connecting trail between the Belly River valley and the Many Glacier region and is frequently travelled in both directions. In the Belly River region, the Ptarmigan Trail departs east from the foot of Cosley Lake (56-57). The Ptarmigan Trail may also be picked up 2.5 km along the Elizabeth Lake Trail (53). In Many Glacier, the Ptarmigan Trail begins at the end of the Swiftcurrent Inn parking lot.

ATTRACTIONS Spectacular high country trail; fine views. Travels through 56-metre (185 ft.) tunnel. Overnight camping at Cosley and Elizabeth lakes. No open fires. Fishing at Cosley, Elizabeth and Ptarmigan lakes.

CONSIDERATIONS Steep uphill climb from Elizabeth Lake or Many Glacier. Travels high, exposed alpine country. Carry extra clothing and see Hypothermia in the introductory section. Snow persists on high sections well into the summer season. Deep snow can accumulate early in fall. Check with a Park ranger for trail conditions. Watch the weather while travelling as visibility is essential for navigation on the upper sections. Turn back if

weather closes in. Gable Mountain and Many Glacier quadrangle maps are recommended. Suspension bridge over Elizabeth Lake outlet removed in early fall and not replaced until late spring; hikers may have to wade the creek. The Ptarmigan Tunnel doors are closed and locked in fall and not re-opened until late June. **HORSES:** Riders should lead their mounts across snow areas and along steep scree sections. Horse travel may not be feasible until July if snow persists. Check with rangers before departing.

THE TRAIL The Ptarmigan Trail leaves Cosley Lake and fords its outflow stream as the trail rises above the Mokowanis River yalley in a few short switchbacks. The trail traverses the north end of Cosley ridge through subalpine forest and enters the Belly River valley. At 3 km the Elizabeth Lake Trail from the Belly River ranger station joins with Ptarmigan to Elizabeth Lake. This section is described under Elizabeth (53).

A signpost at the backcountry campsite on the north end of Elizabeth Lake directs travellers to the continuation of the Ptarmigan which branches left to cross the suspension bridge over the Belly River. A good horse ford is provided here. The climb ahead is steep and travellers may wish to rest before making the demanding ascent. As the trail rises above the valley, openings in the mixed forest reveal an increasingly magnificent view. At 9.5 km the Redgap Pass Trail branches left and climbs 4.1 km to the pass before descending to Kennedy Creek.

From this junction the Ptarmigan Trail soon reaches open scree slopes as it ascends to the tunnel along a trail blasted from steep cliffs that form Ptarmigan Wall. A 56-metre tunnel allows travel through an otherwise impassable ridge. The views along this open section are some of the finest in the Park. As you emerge from the tunnel, an expanse of high mountains and alpine valleys stretches to the southern horizon.

It is another 8.6 km to Many Glacier as the trail begins a steep, quick descent to Ptarmigan Lake which offers good trout fishing. Below the lake 2.6 km, the Ptarmigan Trail meets the Iceberg Lake Trail which branches right to that popular destination. The Ptarmigan Trail continues another 4.3 km to Many Glacier.

56 COSLEY LAKE CUTOFF

Trailhead:	Belly River Ranger Station
Destination:	Northeast shore of Cosley Lake
Length:	3.2 km (2 mi.) allow 1 hr. each away
Difficulty Level:	Moderately easy

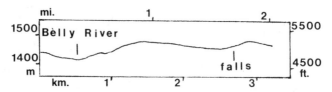

ACCESS The Cosley Lake Cutoff Trail branches right from the Belly River Valley Trail (51) 200 metres from the ranger station. This trail may also be reached from the west via Stoney Indian Pass Trail (57).

ATTRACTIONS Access from the Belly River to Cosley Lake and the Stoney Indian Pass Trail, Gros Ventre Falls. Fishing at Cosley for rainbow, whitefish and lake trout from late May to Nov. 30. Bear Mountain lookout side trail.

CONSIDERATIONS No facilities in this section. Belly River suspension bridge removed in fall and replaced in mid-May. **HORSES:** Early season high water may make river crossing dangerous. Check with Belly River ranger station for conditions.

THE TRAIL This short connecting trail leads from Belly River ranger station to the northeastern shore of Cosley Lake. Hikers travelling out of the Belly River valley into the Mokowanis drainage cross the largest suspension bridge in Glacier Park. A good horse ford is adjacent downstream from the bridge. The trail climbs gently through trees for 2.4 km where a short spur extends left to lovely Gros Ventre Falls. The main trail continues southwest another half kilometre at which point Bear Mountain lookout trail branches right for a steep 2.7 km climb to a lofty overlook, a popular viewpoint.

A short distance beyond this side trail, the main trail reaches Cosley Lake and a major junction. To the left, the Ptarmigan Trail (55) crosses the outflow river from the lake and continues to Elizabeth Lake on its way to Many Glacier. This junction is the terminus of the Cosley Lake Cutoff Trail. Ahead and continuing southwest, the long Stoney Indian Pass Trail (57) climbs up and over the pass to meet the Waterton Valley Trail (62).

57 STONEY INDIAN PASS

Trailhead: Cosley Lake Trail Junction
Destination: Waterton Valley Trail Junction
Length: 24 km (15 mi.) allow 10 to 11 hrs. one way
Difficulty Level: Moderately difficult

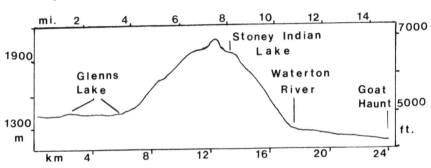

ACCESS From the Belly River area follow the Cosley Lake Cutoff Trail (56) to its junction with the Stoney Indian Trail. The Stoney Trail may also be reached via the Ptarmigan Trail (55) from Many Glacier and the Waterton Valley Trail (62) from Goat Haunt (58).

ATTRACTIONS Spectacular trail into high alpine country. Side trail to Mokowanis Lake. Fishing in Cosley, Glenns and Mokowanis lakes from late May to Nov. 30. Beautiful waterfalls. Stoney Indian Bench, a natural flower garden.

CONSIDERATIONS Trail crosses high mountain pass exposed to wind and sudden weather changes. Be well prepared. Snow pockets remain until late summer. Biting insects in lower Mokowanis and Waterton valleys; carry repellent. Trail around Stoney Indian Lake may be submerged during high water; wading may be necessary. Quadrangle maps needed: Gable Mountain, Mount

Cleveland, Porcupine Ridge, Ahern Pass. If travelled in reverse from the Waterton Valley, climb to Stoney Indian Pass is steep and demanding. **HORSES:** If wading the shore of Stoney Indian Lake, travel slowly as rocky bottom creates tricky footing.

THE TRAIL This high mountain pass has long been used as a travel corridor between the Waterton and Belly River valleys and is named for the Stoney Indians who travelled it to reach hunting and fishing in the Belly River area.

From the Cosley Lake junction, the Stoney Indian Pass Trail follows the lakeshore across open meadows to the Cosley Lake campsite area. From the campsite the Stoney trail continues along the shore of Cosley and crosses an alluvial fan to Glenns Lake. The two lakes were once one, but outwash debris from Kaina Creek has separated them. For the fisherman, a stopover in this area can be worthwhile as both Cosley and Glenns lakes are noted for their rainbow and lake trout.

A backcountry campsite at the foot of Glenns Lake accommodates both hikers and riders in sites with grates for open fires. The trail climbs steeply, rising above the lake and levelling into dense forest which lines the way 4 km to a small hikers' campsite on upper Glenns Lake. Hitch-rails here are a day-use convenience for riders.

A short distance beyond, the Mokowanis Trail branches left (south) passing beneath picturesque White Quiver Falls in its 1.6 km climb to Mokowanis Lake. A hikers' campsite and good fishing make this a popular side trip.

The main trail curves right at the Mokowanis junction. A large campsite here accommodates both hikers and horses. The climb to the pass begins beyond the junction and becomes steep as it leaves the protection of the forest. The magnificence of the surrounding landscape that was screened by a foreground of trees opens up as you rise into the alpine world. The cascades of the upper Mokowanis border the trail to the southeast and the distinctive Pyramid Peak, often dotted with mountain goats, is in the foreground. Well-designed switchbacks assist as you climb to the Atsina Lake basin, a compound cirque. Magnificent waterfalls plunge down the steps of this glacier-carved staircase, the beauty of which becomes more evident as the trail continues the demanding climb to Stoney Indian Pass. Hanging glaciers, gardens of wildflowers and grizzly and mountain goat habitat along the way are all representative of the true alpine.

You will need a rest when you reach the summit at 2100 metres and, on days with no wind, many hours can be spent here exploring the surrounding peaks, glaciers and remote benches with binoculars. Merritt, Cathedral, Ipasha, Kipp and Cleveland are but a few of the giants that reach for the sky here. Climbing routes for Mount Cleveland, the highest in the Parks, depart from this pass. The descent to Stoney Indian Lake is quick and steep. The lake is set between high ridges and offers a sheltered feeling after the open high country. A hikers' campsite is located on the northwest shore; no open fires allowed. The sawtooth crest of Porcupine Ridge is a welcoming landmark as the Stoney trail descends 3.2 km to the wooded Waterton valley and the junction with the Waterton Valley Trail (62) which travels north 7.8 km to Goat Haunt and south 9 km to the Fifty Mountain campsite.

Waterton Valley

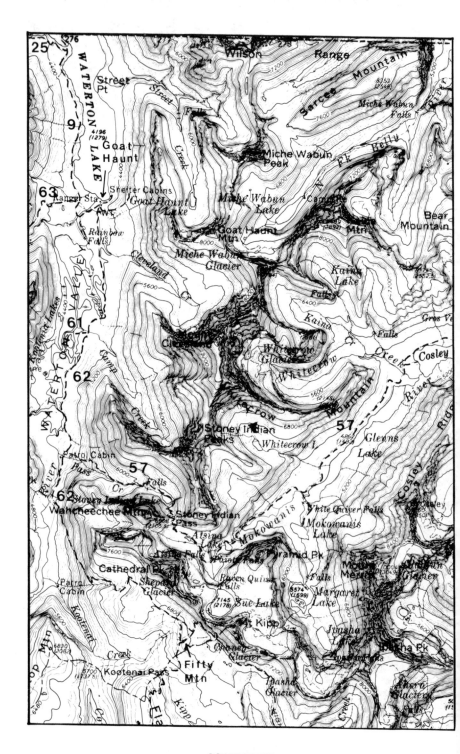

GOAT HAUNT

100

58 GOAT HAUNT

TRAILHEAD FOR:
Goat Haunt Viewpoint (59), Rainbow Falls (60), Kootenai Lakes (61), Waterton Valley (62), Boulder Pass (63) and Waterton Lakeshore (9) trails.

Goat Haunt ranger station at the southern end of Upper Waterton Lake is the backcountry headquarters for Northern Glacier and a popular destination for visitors to Waterton Lakes National Park. Scheduled boats from Waterton townsite provide easy access to this otherwise remote outpost and the Lakeshore (9), Waterton Valley (62) and Boulder Pass (63) trails offer overland routes.

Flanked by the impressive peak of Mount Cleveland to the east and the jagged Citadel Peaks (Porcupine Ridge) to the west, Goat Haunt is a picturesque sight. Covered shelters at the boat dock offer comfortable benches, restrooms and, on cool days, a warming fire in the fireplace. A paved path follows the shoreline a short distance to the ranger station. Information, backcountry permits and area maps are available here as well as an attractive visitor centre and a water fountain. A small staff of rangers and trail crew live in this pleasant spot during the summer.

The lure of the backcountry is strong here and many trails lead out from Goat Haunt to connect with the extensive network of trails that criss-crosses Glacier Park. For the casual walker interested in a leisurely stroll, several short trails explore the surrounding area.

Hikers travelling from or into Canada are subject to customs clearance and identification is required.

A backcountry campground near the mouth of the Waterton River can accommodate both hikers and riders. There are no commercial facilities at Goat Haunt and visitors planning to overnight at the campsite must be fully equipped. Camp shelters at the boat dock are also available for overnight use and are the only accommodation for those who miss the last boat. Enjoy your day, but be sure to leave enough time to get back to the dock before your boat departs.

59 GOAT HAUNT VIEWPOINT

Trailhead: Goat Haunt Ranger Station
Destination: Viewpoint on Goat Haunt Ridge
Length: 1.6 km (1 mi.) allow 1 hr. one way
Difficulty Level: Moderately difficult

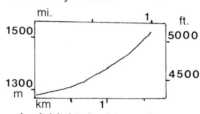

ACCESS The trail branches left behind the bunkhouse at the Goat Haunt ranger station (58).

ATTRACTIONS Fine view of the Waterton valley and Olson Creek drainage. Huckleberries in August.

CONSIDERATIONS Short steep trail. Carry water. Return by same route. No facilities. Porcupine Ridge quadrangle map recommended.

THE TRAIL The climb to the site of an old fire lookout is steep, but the view at the trail's end is well worth the effort. Cool evergreens line the trail as you quickly climb above the valley bottom. As the trees thin to allow a sweeping view of the surrounding area, the beauty of the upper reaches of the Olson Creek valley and the distinctive hoodoos of Porcupine Ridge are more clearly revealed. Tour boats from Waterton townsite 10 km away grow steadily larger as they slowly approach the ranger station below.

Rock outcroppings on the upper reaches of the trail contain several fine examples of colonial algae, the oldest fossils found in the Rockies. These circular groupings lived in the inland sea that covered this entire region before the great upheaval that formed the mountains. Enjoy the summer wildflowers and the August huckleberries as you return to the lakeshore.

60 RAINBOW FALLS

Trailhead: Goat Haunt Ranger Station
Destination: Rainbow Falls
Length: 1.5 km (1 mi.) allow 20 minutes one way
Difficulty Level: Easy

ACCESS To reach Rainbow Falls, follow the trail that branches right (west) approximately 40 metres beyond the ranger station at Goat Haunt (58).

ATTRACTIONS Rainbow Falls cas-

102

cade. Wildlife mineral lick. Access to Waterton River points for good fishing from late May to Nov. 30. Interpretive hikes. Easy-to-reach beargrass habitat.

CONSIDERATIONS   Beyond the ranger station, two trails branch right; stay to the left at both and do not cross the river. Slippery, slanting rocks at the edge of the falls are dangerous; stay back. No facilities. Return by same route. Porcupine Ridge quadrangle map recommended.

THE TRAIL   The short trip to Rainbow Falls offers a backcountry feeling only a mile from the relative civilization of Goat Haunt. As you leave the buildings the chug of the generator fades and the quiet of a mature forests enfolds you. The smell of pine and spruce is in the air and your footsteps are muted by the thick layer of fallen needles on the forest floor. At .5 km the sound of flowing water breaks the stillness as the trail meets the horse ford which branches right (west) to the Lakeshore Trail (9).

Continuing to the left, the trail meets another branch at .9 km. Here the hikers' route to the Lakeshore Trail goes right and over a suspension bridge. The Rainbow Falls Trail swings left and around a small muddy pond. This area is a treat to amateur naturalists as the minerals in the water attract considerable wildlife. Moose, elk, deer and bear are the larger creatures who frequent the area, while mink, marten and wolverine may also be seen. And if there are no animals visible when you are here, tracks in the muddy slough record their passing.

Beargrass comprises part of the forest understory as the trail continues and, a short distance beyond the mineral spring, a boggy pond becomes visible through the trees. Alleys through the pines lead to the edge of this open grassy slough surrounded by dense forest with the towering cliffs of Mount Cleveland as a backdrop. The trail soon meets the Waterton River and continues along its rocky bank to Rainbow Falls. Here the river has carved a channel over and through resistant rock as it cascades into a deep pool below. A dynamic sight at any time, the falls are particularly spectacular in June as the torrent of spring meltwater from high in the mountains roars through this narrow chute.

61 KOOTENAI LAKES

Trailhead:	Goat Haunt
Destination:	Kootenai Lakes
Length:	4.5 km (2.8 mi.) allow 1 to 1½ hrs. one way
Difficulty Level:	Easy

ACCESS   To reach the Kootenai Lakes, follow the Waterton Valley Trail (62) from Goat Haunt ranger station (58) 4 km (2.5 mi.) to the Kootenai Lakes cutoff. The trail branches right (west) .5 km to the lakes. These lakes may also be approached from the south via Waterton Valley Trail from Fifty Mountain or Stoney Indian Pass (57).

ATTRACTIONS   Excellent moose habitat. Brook trout fishing from late May to Nov. 30. Lovely fall hike.

CONSIDERATIONS   Biting insects in summer. This area has been heavily used and unfortunately abused; please be careful and considerate and pack out all that you pack in. Bears frequent the area; fishermen must properly dispose of fish entrails. No open fires at Kootenai campsites. Porcupine quadrangle map suggested.

THE TRAIL   Tall, dense spruce and fir trees canopy the trail most of the way to the lakes. In their shadows are the axe-hewn stumps of trees cut in a logging operation in the early years of this century. As you near the lake, forest gives way to open marshland that typifies this wide valley and fine views of the surrounding peaks are stunning. At 4 km the Kootenai Lakes Trail branches right (west) to the campsite area on the largest of this chain of shallow lakes. Hitchrails here accommodate horse campers.

These lakes are home to variety of wildfowl and are one of the best moose habitats in Glacier Park. The largest member of the deer family, adult bull moose can weigh as much as 1000 lbs. Specially adapted for life in marshy habitat. their long distinctive snout allows them to graze on underwater vegetation and their flexible nostrils can be closed during feeding. Wide-spreading hooves minimize suction and allow them to walk easily on swampy ground and muddy lake and river bottoms. Long legs allow moose to travel easily through deep snows that accumulate in mountain valleys where they winter.

During the mating season in September bull moose can be quite aggressive and care should be taken at that time. The females are noted for their protective behaviour with their calves. Enjoy these impressive wetland animals with respect and understanding.

62 WATERTON VALLEY

Trailhead:	Goat Haunt
Destination:	Fifty Mountain campsites
Length:	16.9 km (10.5 mi.) allows 5 to 6 hrs. one way
Difficulty Level:	Moderately difficult

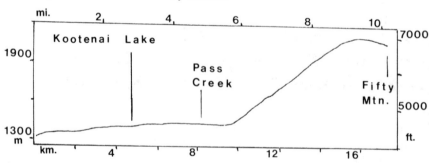

ACCESS The Waterton Valley Trail departs south from the ranger station at Goat Haunt. The trail may also be reached from the Belly River region to the east via the Stoney Indian Pass Trail (57), from the south via the High Line Trail and the West Flattop Trail, from the north along the Lakeshore Trail (9), and from the west via the Boulder Pass Trail (63).

ATTRACTIONS Major travel corridor between Goat Haunt and Logan Pass. Access to Fifty Mountain area and far-reaching views. Excellent wildlife habitat. Wildflowers. Sue Lake overlook.

CONSIDERATIONS Long steady climb that can be very hot in afternoon sun; travel early. Carry insect repellent. Grizzly bears frequent Fifty Mountain area. No open fires at campsites.

THE TRAIL It is a forested hike up the Waterton Valley to the Pass Creek patrol cabin. An early departure (recommended) will take you through cool woods still damp with night dew and a sweater will be welcome. At 4.5 km the Kootenai Lakes

Trail (61) branches right (west) and a quick side trip along this short spur may be rewarded with the sight of moose feeding in the morning sun. The Waterton Valley Trail continues south to the junction with the Stoney Indian Pass Trail (57) at 7.8 km. A short distance further across the Pass Creek footbridge, the trail arrives at the Pass Creek patrol cabin. Cool shade alongside a mountain stream makes a pleasant spot to snack and rest for the long steady climb ahead. A mile beyond the cabin the trail reveals its second nature as it leaves the trees and rises above the Waterton River. This section crosses open avalanche swaths and rock ledge outcroppings as it makes one long strenuous traverse to the Fifty Mountain plateau. It is a demanding uphill slog and can be extremely hot and dry if travelled in the afternoon sun.

As the trail breaks onto the wide, flat expanse of subalpine meadow carpeted with mountain grasses and flowers, the strenuous trip receives its just reward. The ragged snow-covered peaks that can be seen in every direction are a stark constrast to the lush garden-like setting at your feet. Travellers may wish to linger here with their flower guides and topographical maps identifying species and peaks. The Waterton Valley Trail continues directly to the Fifty Mountain campsite set in the southeast corner of the meadow.

A major trail junction, Fifty Mountain is the terminus of the Waterton Valley Trail. Continuing south along the base of Mount Kipp, the High Line Trail follows the Continental Divide to Granite Park Chalet at 19 km and to Logan Pass, another 12 km. The West Flattop Trail leaves Fifty Mountain campsite and heads south through forest and meadow to Packers Roost in the McDonald Valley.

Travellers on the High Line Trail and Fifty Mountain campers who would enjoy a side trip might explore the Sue Lake overlook. This short, steep trek scrambles .6 km to the crest for an extraordinary view into the Sue Lake basin and the Mokowanis valley beyond. The trail branches east from the High Line Trail above the Fifty Mountain campsite.

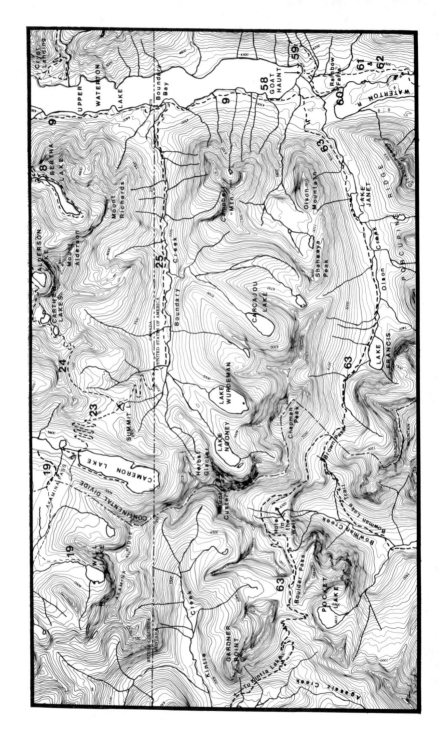

BOULDER PASS

63 BOULDER PASS

Trailhead: Goat Haunt
Destination: Boulder Pass
Length: 21.2 km (13.2 mi.) allow 7 to 9 hrs. one way
Difficulty Level: Moderately difficult

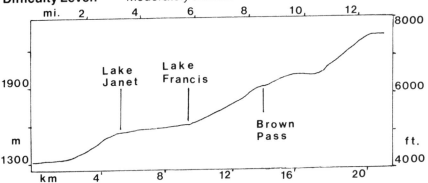

ACCESS From Goat Haunt, follow the Rainbow Falls Trail (60) that departs right (west) 40 metres beyond the ranger station. At .9 km branch right to join the Lakeshore Trail (9) and cross the Waterton River on a suspension bridge. At .5 km beyond the bridge, the Boulder Pass Trail branches left (west). **HORSES:** The horse ford trail branches right from the Rainbow Falls Trail .5 km along the trail and joins the Lakeshore Trail to the Boulder Pass Trail as above.

Boulder Pass may also be reached from the North Fork area of Glacier Park. From Kintla Lake ranger station, follow the Boulder Pass Trail 20.1 km to Boulder Pass. From Bowman Lake, follow the Bowman Lake Trail 22.2 km to Brown Pass and the junction with Boulder Pass Trail.

ATTRACTIONS Splendid high alpine trail. Travels remote, recently-glaciated high basin territory. Beautiful wildflowers. Good fishing for rainbow trout at Lake Francis from late May to Nov. 30. Exposed pillow lava.

CONSIDERATIONS Travel into high alpine country and across exposed mountain pass. Fast-changing weather; cold and wind are possible at any time. Be prepared. Section from Brown Pass to Upper Kintla Lake should not be attempted in bad weather or on days with poor visibility as visual navigation is necessary on steep, narrow sections. Extreme vertical exposure on sections of upper trail. Snowfields remain until late season. Quarangle maps needed: Porcupine Ridge, Mount Carter, Kintla Peak. Store salty boots, clothing and horse tack securely as deer and mountain goats hungry for salt may be attracted.

HORSES: Riders should lead horses across steep, narrow section above Brown Pass. Horse travel may be impossible until mid-August. Check with Park ranger for conditions.

THE TRAIL Travellers along the Boulder Pass Trail begin and end their alpine adventure in the dense forests of lowland lake valleys. Thick forest shelters the trail as it rises quickly 5.6 km to Lake Janet. A large boulder field at the lakeshore is the result of a massive rock slide from Olson Mountain which dammed the creek and created this shallow lake. Mudflats at the upper end of the lake record animal tracks and make for an interesting stop. A small campground accommodates hikers and riders; no open fires are permitted.

As the trail penetrates farther up the valley, high peaks close in, their slopes striped with the light green of avalanche tracks and darker green of coniferous forests. Splintered trees tell of the power of avalanches. At 10 km a short spur trail branches left to the shore of Lake Francis, a popular destination with fishermen. Unmarked paths extend around the lake, and care should be taken on the slippery rock ledges above the deep, icy water. Set against the vertical cliffs of The Sentinel, a waterfall spills down from Dixon Glacier into the lake. On windy days the falls scarcely reach their base as powerful updrafts catch the misty water and send it upward again.

A short climb above Francis the Boulder Pass Trail reaches the Hawksbill campsite, open to hikers only. Open fires are not permitted. Above the campsite, the trail enters the subalpine world and wildflowers and shrubs replace the dense forest for the remaining climb to Brown Pass, 13.8 km from Goat Haunt. Brown is a wide pass contained to the south by Thunderbird Mountain cradling its glacier in steep cliff arms. The Bowman Lake Trail branches left at this summit on its 22.2 km journey through the valley below. This route is a good alternative if the weather turns bad, and is also useful for riders in early summer.

Beyond Brown Pass the alpine journey takes on fantastic proportions. As the trail branches right and takes to the slopes of Chapman Peak, the surrounding expanse of towering, glacier-laden peaks is revealed as the green ribbon of the Bowman valley with its long blue lake extends 2000 feet below. The trail narrows as it creeps along a sheer rock wall. At 16.6 km a spur trail drops down to Hole-in-the-Wall campsite situated in a staircase cirque carved from Mount Custer. A small meadow in the cirque is a paradise in this rock world. Peppered with dwarf fir and larch, it is a patchwork of alpine wildflowers during the blooming season, considered by many to be the finest display in Glacier Park. Waterfalls pour into the basin, creating a constant chorus of water on stone. This high country is home to the grizzly; and mule deer, mountain goats, porcupines and wolveries also frequent this beautiful arena. No horse camping or open fires are permitted in this fragile alpine environment.

Goats may be companions as the Boulder Pass Trail arcs high above the Hole-in-the-Wall basin toward the pass summit. The trail ascends through an unusual outcropping pillow lava. A rare geological site, the layer of Purcell lava was excreted into water when this area was an inland sea millions of years ago, forming peculiar shapes that were later scoured and polished by glacial action. The remaining outcroppings are yet another fascinating feature of this trail.

The rest of the distance to Boulder Pass crosses a recently-glaciated area. Less than 20 years ago, the trail skirted the lower extent of the Boulder Glacier which filled the approach to the pass and has now retreated to a higher perch. A relatively new route travels across this glaciated path and the scars of glacial action are obvious and numerous. This new route presents an easy walkway to the pass and views from this lofty perch are superb.

Below Boulder Pass to the west a campsite accommodates hikers, but no open fires are allowed in this delicate environment. Fine alpine flowers and stands of larch add color here, a stark contrast to the ice and rock of the pass. Porcupines can be a problem and care should be taken to store sweaty clothes and boots out of reach of these salt-loving creatures. From the Boulder Pass campground, it is a quick, steep descent to the forested valley for the 20 km hike to the Kintla ranger station.

SELECTED REFERENCES

The following books are some which we found useful. Those marked * are recommended to readers who would like to know more about their subject matter than we have been able to include in this guide, and are currently available from the Waterton Natural History Association.

Anderson, R.S. and Donald, D.B. *Limnological Survey of Waterton Lakes National Park*, prepared for Parks Canada by Canadian Wildlife Service, Calgary, 1976, unpublished.

Beaumont, Greg. *Many-storied Mountains: The Life of Glacier National Park*, National Park Services, U. S. Department of the Interior, Washington, D.C., 1978, 138 pp.

* Craighead, J.J., Craighead, F.C. Jr., and Davis, R.J. *A Field Guide to Rocky Mountain Wildflowers*, Houghton Mifflin Company, Boston, 1963, 275 pp.

* Djuff, Ray, ed. Chris Morrison, *A History of the Prince of Wales Hotel*, Waterton Natural History Association, 1991, 50 pp.

* Gadd, Ben, *Handbook of the Canadian Rockies*, Corax Press, Jasper, Alta., 876 pp.

Harrison, John E. *Evolution of a Landscape: The Quarternary Period in Waterton Lakes National Park*, Geological Survey of Canada, Ottawa, 1976, 33 pp. and map.

* Herrero, Stephen, *Bear Attacks*, Hurtig Publishers, Edmonton, 1985, 287 pp.

McArthur, K.L. *About Bears*, Glacier Natural History Association, pamphlet.

* Nelson, Dick and Sharon, *Hiker's Guide to Glacier National Park*, Tecolote Press, Inc. Glenwood, N.M., 1978, 111 pp.

* On, Danny and Shaw, Richard J. *Plants of Waterton-Glacier National Parks*, Summerthought, Banff, Alberta, 1979, 160 pp.

* Peterson, Roger Tory. *A Field Guide to Western Birds*, Houghton Mifflin Company, Boston, 1990, 309 pp.

* Pringle, Heather, *Waterton Lakes National Park*, Douglas & McIntyre, Vancouver, B.C., 1986, 127 pp.

* Raup, O.B., Carhart, R.L., Whipple, J.W. and Carrara, P.E. *Geology Along Going-to-the-Sun Road, Glacier Park*, Glacier Natural History Association, West Glacier, Mont., 1983, 62 pp. and map.

* Robbins, Chandler S.; Bruun, Bertzel; Zim, Herbert S. *Birds of North American*, H.D. Fenn and Company Ltd., Mississauga, Ont., 1983, 360 pp.

* Robbins, Michael. *Along the Continental Divide*, National Geographic Society, Washington, D.C., 1981, 200 pp.

* Rodney, William. *Kootenai Brown: His Life and Times*, Gray's Publishing Ltd., Sidney B.C., 1969, 251 pp.

* Scotter, George W., Halle Flygare, *Wildflowers of the Canadian Rockies*, Hurtig Publishers, Edmonton, 1986, 170 pp.

Taylor, John. *Trail Inventory: Waterton Lakes National Park*, 1977.

Williams, M.B. *Waterton National Park*, Historic Trails Society of Alberta, 1982, 48 pp. and map.

INDEX

NOTES